TAKING A CITY

TAKING A CITY

BY

DOUGLAS HORTON

HARPER & BROTHERS PUBLISHERS
New York and London

CONTENTS

67028

TAKING A CITY

TAKING A CITY

A Sermon for the Builders of the City of God

*"There was found a poor wise man, and he by
his wisdom delivered the city."*

ECCL. 9:15

OVER against us looms this magnificent and terrible city
of Chicago.

> Hog Butcher for the World,
>   Tool Maker, Stacker of Wheat,
> Player with Railroads and the Nation's Freight Handler
>   Stormy, husky, brawling,
> City of the Big Shoulders. . . .[1]

Our problem is how to convert this city, stupendous
as it is, into the still more stupendous city of God. If
only there could be found the poor wise man of Ecclesiastes who would tell us how! What is the wisdom
whereby he might deliver us from our present, build
us up to the height of our spiritual capacity, and present
us to the future the living embodiment of the ideal society of men? How shall we make the city not merely

[1] From "Chicago" in *Chicago Poems*, by Carl Sandburg. By
permission of the publisher, Henry Holt and Co.

hog butcher, tool maker, and an emporium for commerce, but also a reservoir of humanity at its best, a city which clothes all of its citizens in faith, a city where the good life is lived naturally and all men know the meaning of liberty and loyalty? How, in a word, shall we impart a soul to Chicago?

We need a Bible.—In lieu of the poor wise man, who today seems conspicuously absent, we shall have to turn to the historians to ask when cities or other communities of human beings have been at their dynamic mightiest. A first answer they might give is a strange one: people spiritually mighty have usually—perhaps always—been people of a book. They have been people who have accustomed themselves to look to a book for the revelation of God's will: from it they have expected him to speak to them. Surely it is not without significance that of the twelve historical religions which are dead—the ancient Egyptian, the Peruvian and Mexican, Mithraism, Manichæism, the Babylonian, Phœnician, and Hittite, the Greek, the Roman, the early Teutonic and Scandinavian —not one of them, according to Robert Ernest Hume, "possessed anything which might be called a canon of sacred Scriptures," whereas every one of the eleven living religions—Hinduism, Jainism, Buddhism, Sikhism, Confucianism, Taoism, Shinto, Judaism, Zoroastrianism, Mohammedanism, and Christianity—"do possess definite sets of documents which are regarded as conveying unique

divine truths which need to be known." There is power
in the Book from which God speaks.

And what if the Book happens to be that crown of
all the others, the Book in which it is set down that the
God who is speaking is not the God merely of this tribe
or that cult, but the Father of every human individual
born into the world! *That* Book was rediscovered at
the dawn of the Reformation after its long sleep in
Latin. Wycliffe's translation into English, though only
in manuscript, swept like earthquake tremors through
the kingdom, and with something like the same results.
A considerable sum was paid even for a few sheets of it;
a load of hay became the price for permission to read in
it one hour a day for a period; and some learned sections
of it by heart to recite to the throngs who gathered to
hear. The readers of it went to their death when cap-
tured by the authorities, who were afraid of the power
of it: they were hunted down like wild beasts and burned
with copies of it round their necks. But the Bible won
its own way; it changed the lives of those who listened
for God's word in it; eventually it revolutionized
Europe.

The arresting fact about our situation here—a fact
which sends one's thought of the future soaring—is that a
new book of the Bible has been discovered in our day and
God speaks from it as dreadfully and graciously as ever
he spoke from Job or St. John. The book newly discovered is nothing else than *the city of Chicago itself.*

(3)

Hitherto, for the most part, cities have been regarded only as cities; and to most of our fellow citizens Chicago is only a city. But we have learned that it is more. It is a scripture, an inspired scripture being written before our eyes by the awful hand of the Almighty and communicating to us his will. What he is writing is strangely like what he has already written in his other books, now printed. "He that takes the sword—or gun—shall perish by it"—can one miss that oft-repeated text inscribed across the gangster areas? "I have made of one blood all nations of men, and belligerency between races means disaster for all"—something written in our streets in a clearer hand than writing. And as one walks through the canyon of La Salle Street, is there not posted on a score of windows, whence men in despair have flung themselves, the dark legend, "What shall it profit a man if he gain the whole world and lose his soul?" This city is a Bible from the pages of which God is speaking.

The importance of the Sacred Book has never lain in its being a book as such: the significant matter is that people have come to look there for a revelation of God's purpose. It is just this that may make the book of Chicago infinitely momentous. I am mistaken if this new and daring trait we are developing—that of holding before our eyes the flaming pages of this canonical book called Our City and asking God what he means by it—does not have upon us the same effect of shock, contrition, amaze, and release to our higher capacities as had the open Bible of Wycliffe upon the people of his day.

We need a Bible and we have it.

We need a Bible with a Gospel in it.—The historians would go on to point out, I have no doubt, that the human spirit rises to its height when it has in its possession a myth, a story about God. The spirit of the greater cities of the ancient world was almost always invested in a myth. Was not every king of Memphis the bodily son of Re, the sun god of old Egypt? Did not the fall of the statue of Diana from the skies establish the existence of the temple and city of Ephesus? Did not Athena contest with Poseidon the privilege of directing the destiny of Athens? Did not the owl-eyed goddess, offering peace and prosperity, win the privilege from the ruler of the deep, who had only war to offer? And did not the art and prowess of Athens owe more than today can be computed to the belief of the people in their myth?

But when a myth is true and verifiable, when it tells the story of God coming into the world to redeem it, then it becomes a Gospel that sets the world aquiver with joyous faith and gratitude. It was the true myth, the Gospel, the story of what God had actually done, which, on the lips of the Reformers, remade the then world. Always the church is in danger of slipping into the imperative mood in its teaching: do this or do that, and you shall be saved. It is a mood which puts the emphasis on the work of men—a tragic mood, therefore, since no man can save himself without God. It is not the mood of myth. What the Reformers did was to restore to the church her ancient and thrilling indicative: this *has* been willed and that *has* been done by the Almighty and you *are* saved. *Sola gratia*—by grace alone—by grace alone the world is overcome. And through grace the Reformers did indeed overcome their world.

Nor is this city without its myth. To some it may be, but not to us. It contains a fifth Gospel, the story of what God has actually done and how he has done it. It would not be a creditable Bible unless it held a Gospel. It is the Gospel quality that characterizes many men and women in it whom I could name. They are living announcements not primarily that God might act or should act, but that he has acted: he has reached into history and taken them for his purposes; there is an unbroken historical chain which unites God and Christ and them. Every significant person in history has had a mythical aura about him; you cannot account for them in terms of history alone; and of none may this be said more truly than of the disciples of Christ who labor in this city—in its slums and in its high places. Whence have these servants of God the motive to build upon the insight that all men are brothers? To go out on the streets and call into their hospitality drunkards and nameless wretches who never did and never would have any claim upon them? To challenge the citizens to study and think their way into nobler living? Or to heal minds broken in distraction over many things by illuminating to them the one thing needful? Did the motive for this kind of living come from materialism and animal selfishness? It came from a lovely place; it came, by a direct route, from the heart of the Eternal. Here is a story about what God has *done*. Here is the Gospel.

We need a Bible with a Gospel in it, and that, if we will look for it, is also to be found in this Chicago.

We need a Bible with a Gospel in it and the power of the resurrection in that Gospel.—An eschatology is a doctrine about the last things. It was such a doctrine that gave Buddhism its fascination for millions in its heyday; follow the Buddha in his fourfold path and you come to the end of this torture misnamed existence. It is such a doctrine that gives Mohammedanism its savage beauty. It is something to know that if you die fighting for the faith your soul flies instantly to Paradise. One moment the clash of steel or the clangor of the guns; the next the quiet streams and restful gardens of eternity. It is this belief that has made the pious Moslem, throughout his history, unconquerable in battle, save when he was overwhelmed by the sheer numbers or better military equipment of the enemy.

There have been freakish kinds of Christianity which, though they emphasized distorted views of their own triumph at time's imminent end, did yet reveal what immense control such a belief has over a person. From the time of the Montanists who gathered at Pepuza in Asia Minor in the second century to await the end of the world to the time of the Russellite neighbors of mine who not long ago banded together in a kind of Christian communism awaiting the same cataclysm, this doctrine that something in the nature of an end is about to happen, from which believers shall somehow enjoy redemption, has been powerful to challenge men and women to their highest spiritual daring.

But in true Christianity mere eschatology, the general doctrine of the nearness of heaven, potent as that is, becomes what St. Paul called the *power of the resurrection*. This is the power possessed by every man and woman who takes for granted the immortality of the soul, and then proceeds to live in the knowledge that this life does not exhaust his possibilities. Immediately you see what happens: such people sit loose to the circumstances of this existence, but have a firm grip on the things that are eternal. They become channels by which the heavenly graces may be transmitted to their times. They believe in the power of love, for they know it is the power of heaven. They are not thrown down and engulfed by the weltering hatreds and unhappy changefulness of this world. They know that today we are approaching the end of an age—possibly the *débâcle* of the race—but they are not paralyzed by fears nor made mad by despair. They salute the end. Christianity has never been afraid of the end. They recognize a crisis as the judgment of God making way for his kingdom. Theirs is different from the eschatology of those who looked for a cataclysmic end; they know that even change is evolutionary, gradual. But they are like them in this, that they know that the redemption of God can triumph over any end.

Here then is a Christian sociology tremendous in its implications. It is the sociology of those who believe that the last fact of life is heaven. It is that belief that lends direction and shape and drive to their work on earth. They are realists, but realists with a deathless motive.

Their attitude is slightly though not greatly different from that of Emerson., who, when a millennialist rushed up to him and said, "Mr. Emerson, the world is coming to an end," responded, "Very well, madam, we'll get along without it." For they do not wish to get along without a world; it is simply that they know that their heavenly Gospel does not change with the changes of this world. Let capitalism go, let socialism come and go, let any other doctrine rule—the Gospel of Christ is the same yesterday, today, and forever.

We need a Bible with a Gospel in it, and the power of the resurrection in that Gospel—and all this is to be found, if we will look in the lives of Christ's true disciples, in Chicago.

We need a Bible with a Gospel in it and the power of the resurrection in that Gospel—and an army of saints to declare that power.—The few are important and are a beginning: but they are not enough for the redemption of this vast city. Where is the army of saints to take this city for Christ? That army is here potentially; surely it can be none other than the great body of lay men and lay women of our churches.

One has a feeling that the day of saints has gone by, like that of the trilobites and great auks. We are inclined to think that we live in an era wholly different from that of St. Paul and the early apostles, and that the people they addressed as saints gave their days to prayer and their nights to meditation with a single-mindedness to which we do not even aspire. But if this is our idea, and we are happy in it, we had best be warned against reading the New Testament carefully.

It is a too illuminating exercise to name over the persons we have become accustomed to think of as saints belonging more to heaven than earth, and then to attach to each one the actual description given of him in the records. Matthew turns out to be not a Gabriel sitting on the clouds, but a man who earned his daily bread by collecting taxes. Mark was a private secretary; Luke a physician. John, James, and Peter were engaged in the fish industry. Paul was a manufacturer; Timothy and Titus expert organizers; Jude a small landowner; and Philemon the possessor of an enviable list of well-diversified securities.

There are your first-century saints! They were men—and women—of flesh and blood like yourselves, who had their work to do in this workaday world, but who had also a first-hand interest in the Church, and the worship of God and the moral character in an immoral world that the Church stood for. It was lay men and lay women and not lay angels who, being laid hold of by the Christian ideal, altered the course of destiny for the Roman Empire and so for our Western World.

We might have guessed this, to be sure, from our general knowledge of history, for it was ever so. The great eras of the Christian Church were, as Dean Hodges used to say, those of the missionaries, the monks, and the Methodists—and these were lay movements, movements of the Church as a whole, every one of them. By the missionaries he meant those quiet citizens of the first Christian century who spread the influence of Christ through the whole Roman world, to the extent that Aristides, making his defense before the Emperor Antoninus Pius, could say, "They are to your empire, Your August Highness, what a man's soul is to a man!" By the monks he meant the Franciscans: he thought of Francis himself, the young member of an importing house, who saw materialism and the commercial motive resting like a blight on Europe, and was shocked into action at the sight: who brought to the nations a new spirit by remembering those whom the rest had forgotten, the poor, the leprous, the oppressed, and with others like himself ushered in a century which some critics call the most spacious and magnificent the human race has ever seen. By the Methodists he meant the citizens of town and country in England, rough and refined, in all walks of life, who, a hundred and twenty-five years ago, being emboldened to make their lives count for something more than cash, organized and taught the local "class meetings," as they were called, which brought to half the world a moral revolution felt to this day.

The priests and preachers, prophets and parsons, are very well in their way. To them is delegated supervision, necessary to any organization of people. But if lay initiative, intelligence, and consecration is lacking, they are like to become voices in Rama, producing nothing more substantial than tears. Vitality in a community is not a voice, in any case: it is a condition of rugged health suffusing the whole fabric.

And here all about us are men and women who, if their hearts were touched into flame, could supply that health: they could do as much for our city as ever missionary, monk, or Methodist did for theirs. We need a Bible with a Gospel in it and the power of the resurrection in that Gospel—and in the lay men and lay women of our churches we have an army of saints to declare that power and take the city for Christ.

Men and women of the pews: leaders of the life of our city: it is to you that in the last analysis we must turn. We have the Bible—Chicago itself—through which God is speaking: we have the Gospel, which is the story about God told in the lives of Christ's disciples: we have the power of the resurrection in those lives here among us: but without you the city cannot grow to be the city of God.

But with you, to what future may we not aspire? If you will take seriously your opportunities as citizens of the city of our dream, if you will put by the cheap standards of our present surroundings, if week after week you will draw down from heaven and implant in your work heaven's standards of honesty and fair dealing, sympathy and creativity, I can prophesy a flood time of spiritual power for this city such as today one cannot even conceive.

It is because of you that one can have faith to think of the city with Sandburg,[2]

Under the smoke, dust all over his mouth, laughing with white
    teeth,
Under the terrible burden of destiny laughing as a young man
    laughs. . . .

[2] *Ibid.*

II

"I WAS THERE WHEN THEY CRUCIFIED MY LORD"

A Sermon for Those who are Tired of the Struggle Against Evil

And Jesus entered into Jerusalem.
MARK 11:11

IN THE days of ancient Rome the highest military honor that could be obtained by a general was the triumph by which he celebrated the victory he had won and the power he had achieved over his enemies. He entered the city in a chariot drawn by four horses, preceded by his captives and spoils and followed by his army. With this escort he passed through the streets leading to the Capitol, where he sacrificed a beast to the god of victory.

The pathos of Jesus' triumphal ride into the city of Jerusalem lies in its one vivid contrast to the Roman scene. There were many contrasts, it is true: Jesus was celebrating no victory past, but a victory to come; he was preceded by no slaves or spoils, followed by no army; he rode not on a horse-drawn chariot, but on the humblest burden-bearing animal of the farm. But the one overwhelmingly tragic contrast was that whereas the Roman general knew he was entering a career of high privileges, the Jewish carpenter knew he was riding to his death.

> Ride on, ride on in majesty!
> In lowly pomp ride on to die.
>
> Ride on, ride on in majesty!
> The wingèd squadrons of the sky
> Look down with sad and wondering eyes
> To see the approaching sacrifice.

It was no dumb beast that was to be sacrificed. Jesus knew that the death that was in store was for himself and no other.

Here was a new way to face an evil day—to ride in triumph toward it!

What would you have done? Or perhaps the better question is, What *do* you do when you know you will have to face an evil situation—when, for instance, you know that tomorrow morning you cannot escape finding at your office in these troubled times what amounts to a kind of death in life?

Most of us, to be sure, give ourselves chiefly to *forgetting* the evils that confront us in the world.

Go to any psychiatrist. Ask him what it is that chiefly drives people to seek his aid. Go to Dr. Peabody of Boston, for instance, from whom I quote a case in brief:

He was a man in early middle life who had followed the country-club crowd until for the last years he had been so thoroughly soaked in alcohol as hardly to have drawn a sober breath. Dr. Peabody cured him by basing his diagnosis on one proposition, that the man was *afraid of life*. The trouble was not originally physical, though it had become so. In a sense it was not mental; it was a sickness of spiritual attitude; he had unconsciously set out to forget life and its difficulties, so he had gone through endless routines of superficialities—devoted himself to "going places," the forlorn excitements of extra-marital relationships, and finally to drink. Anything to be relieved of reality! He might have plunged madly into business. He might have taken up one of the false types of religion which are really escapes from life. But the course he actually followed was that of one of his parents, from whom he had learned both fear and the medicine for fear—the medicine that poisons, alcohol.

The relief from one's fears, conscious or unconscious, which is given by alcohol or entertainment or excessive activity, carries with it a thousandfold more of troubles than it narcotizes, for it is at best only temporary, and in every case eats into the basis of one's personality. When, under the touch of a wise psychologist or a friendly friend, a man who has sold his soul for artificial protection from his fears wakes up to see himself as he really is, he knows the terrible inner meaning of Jesus' story of the person who, having one demon in his soul, woke up to find that it had taken in seven other demons more evil than itself. You may contrive to forget the evil that stalks you, but it will not forget you.

This road leads to despair, and often to suicide; by taking to *it* do not think to end your depression: it is not the road that Jesus took on Palm Sunday morning. On that morning he was not carousing with the fishermen on the quay of Tiberius; he was not, as Renan suggests, idling his time away with dark-eyed beauties of Capernaum who might have consented to love him; he was not forgetting life or trying to forget it; he was riding into that Jerusalem in which he knew evil awaited him.

There is another popular method of standing off evil. The psychologists have a name for it, but it is always the method of getting rid of evil by explaining it away. It is believed that one can protect himself from evil if he understands it thoroughly—if he understands its place in the very nature of things.

Explanation always seems to give a sense of happiness. Once you have come to understand the binomial theorem, elementary algebra has no more terrors for you. Once you have learned the lore of the forest, the night noises no longer frighten your slumbers. So, it is said, once you see the meaning of evil, it really ceases to be evil and can be lived with quite comfortably.

If we could only see the whole picture of life, the evil in it would be perceived to be the means for effecting something good later. So runs one explanation. Watch these two men, for instance. They catch a little animal, tie it so that it lies helpless, and while its eyes are still bright and its heart pulsing with life, sever the skin and the muscle wall with a knife, cut into or off, or otherwise alter the action of, the organs within—and callously await results. An indignant protest bursts from us: Stop that! This is sheer cruelty! But, no. These two men are physicians who by this, the only possible method, are isolating the source of the secretion which, when lacking, leaves men and animals to a dreadful death. Their discovery leads eventually to the saving of the lives of hundreds of thousands of men, women, and children. It is pointed out that our appraisal of the physicians' work as evil was immature, rash, and wrong. They were not tormenting the little creature for the love of it; theirs was a larger purpose which made the deed rational, even kind.

So, it is said, the evil endured by people avails always for the salvation of others. Arnold von Winkelried, taking the spears of the enemy into his own bosom, prepares a pathway to liberty for his "children." Captain Oates, walking into the Antarctic desolation, leaves his companions food enough for them to struggle on longer than if he were with them. By these men suffering was voluntarily assumed, as it is wont to be by men and women of heroic cast. But even when it is not, but is laid as a burden on unwilling shoulders, it has a redemptive value.

Had it not been for the agony of the slaves which Lincoln saw in his youth, there would have been no Emancipation Proclamation in 1862. The pain of the few relieves the many.

With these or similar thoughts in their minds some people are able to take the facts of evil calmly. This is especially true if there is a dash of religion in the argument. Let men bring all the evil they may into the world: it will all redound to good in the end; even the wrath of men shall praise the Lord. There is a woman living in a small town in one of our United States who for years has been afflicted with an unhappy disease. Will she go to a physician to have it cured? Not she! "God knows what he is about, and he will bring good out of this," she says to those who remonstrate with her. So she lives with her own malady—and does so, one is bound to add, with creditable equanimity. It seems a far cry from her to any so-called hard-headed business man, but the distance is not overlong between her and the man who says of the present depression: "These things come and go. The only thing to do is to wait this one out. Some good will doubtless come of it. You look at the business curve for the last hundred years; you will see that it goes up and down, down and up. The best way to look at any depression is to regard it as the period which has to precede an era of prosperity."

So, with one explanation or another, we are likely to make peace with the world as it is. But one reason why today I am suspicious that this way of meeting evil cannot be the right one is that I do not find Christ anywhere postulating a theory of evil and being content with it. On Palm Sunday morning he was not sitting down with a group of friends discussing the situation: "Yes, times are bad; the Romans here are gouging every penny of taxes out of us that they can; the whole world is as selfish as can be; a cloud of evil lies over the whole scene; but that is the way things are—good comes out of evil in the long run; it is the part of the philosopher to wait." No, he was not sitting there nor was he saying those words. He was riding into Jerusalem toward Good Friday.

You have doubtless already marked the fallacy that lies at the basis of the attempt to defeat evil by explaining it away. It is the fallacy of mere assent. It is the fallacy of adhering to a theology instead of committing oneself to a discipleship. It is the fallacy of believing that when one has thought a thing out, there is nothing further to do. It is the fallacy of forgetting that thought is nothing more than a faculty to help us *live*.

Good does not arise out of evil mechanically, as smoke from a fire. The cutting up of a little animal does not of itself work the cure of diabetes. That comes only because Dr. Banting and Dr. Best have determined that it shall. Von Winkelried and Oates bring good out of evil because they recognize the latter as evil: it is not

"somehow good" to them in itself: it is only their will
to make good come out of it that brings out any good
whatsoever. There were millions of slaves before Lincoln's time torn from their homes, beaten till bloody, and
hounded until they died, who brought forth no Emancipation Proclamation. It was only when Lincoln saw the
evil as evil and *dedicated* himself to exterminating it that
it could be called the occasion of good. I do not know
what good any economic depression can bring forth of
itself: I see only undernourished children, broken homes,
distracted women, desperate men. Good can ensue only
if some new Lincoln will arise and say, "I'll hit the forces
that produced this and I'll hit them hard." Christ's death
on the cross has no mechanical saving power. It is only
when we ourselves perceive in the cross what happens
to our best when evil goes unrestrained that we are saved
—only when we are stung by it into taking the side of
Christ, opening our hearts to God, and begging to be
used for the extirpation of evil. What made Jesus the
Christ, what made that Syrian peasant the acknowledged
king that he is, was that when he saw the evil of his
day, he recognized in himself the channel of God's grace
to overcome it. He rode to challenge it in Jerusalem.

It is not hard to see how he overcame evil with good.
It is the one way in which we shall lead an overcoming
life.

Evil is a contagion, traveling from person to person. This can be marked in the larger canvas of history. The evil of negro slavery spread gradually over the Western World like a plague. The evil of gangdom has spread gradually over our cities under the mist of our indifference until it has become a national evil. We have seen race prejudice pass from nurse to child, from child to man, from man to community, from community to country, unarrested. And in the smaller world in which each of us lives, we have seen a wrong spawn its impure broods, passion begetting retaliation, retaliation begetting hate, hate begetting anger, and so on to the hundredth vicious generation.

What Jesus did was to let each chain of wrong, when it reached him, come to an end in him. In our West it sometimes happens that a stream that comes down from the snows of the ranges rolls turbulently out of a valley in the foothills and finally disappears from sight where the plains drink it in. Sometimes the streams run through the badlands and are colored with the poisonous-looking greens and yellows of the deposit, until these are lost in the shining white sand. So evil lost itself in the soul of Christ. Anger boiled on its course toward him, but never continued as anger. It disappeared; it exhausted itself in his heart. The poisons of wrong never passed through and issued from him in the colors of retaliation. They were absorbed in the whiteness of his soul.

In order to discover how different he was from the ordinary run of us, and what we need to cultivate in order to overcome evil, it is necessary for us only to re-write the Bible at certain points. Touch up the twenty-third chapter of Luke, for instance, with the spirit of our day, and see how it comes out:

> And the whole company of them rose up and brought him before Pilate. And they began to accuse him, saying, We found this man perverting our nation. And Herod with his soldiers set him at naught and mocked him. And they came unto the place which is called The Skull: there they crucified him. And Jesus said, Damn these men: I'll get them yet!

(For that was really the natural thing to say.)

But what did Jesus really say?

"Father, forgive them: for they know not what they do!"

God has given to you and me that same power of annihilating the trains of evil in our day. I do not know to what you attribute the present depression, whether to selfishness or fear or unbridled competition or what not, but it is clear that the call today is for men and women whose souls are great enough to receive the gangrenous streams that are running through the hearts of men, to receive them and never let them issue forth again. To bear the brunt of selfishness, to feel the wash of hysteria, to admit them to our hearts, and there to abolish them from life! Strange God of power, that thou shouldst have given to us the power to administer eternal death to evil!

He rode into Jerusalem with his heart open to receive all the evils that be, there to let them die.

But he was not merely a negative figure. Goodness also is a contagion. We have seen the goodness which was in Christ caught from heart to heart as a lovely song is caught by one lip from another. Under its spell the first disciples shouted their Hosanna in the Highest and carried through the whole Mediterranean empire their song of triumphant gladness. The cathedral-builders heard it, and the arches, aisles, and storied windows of Paris and Ulm, Siena and Salisbury, rose to its music like the walls of Thebes. The builders of the modern world heard it, and the hospital came into being, and the neighborhood house, the school and the public charity—every institution where the positive love of Christ is dispensed.

That he let flow out upon the world a creative stream of active goodness is made clear enough from a rewriting of the Bible in almost any chapter of the Gospels. Consider the effect of the thirteenth of John if it were in the following form, as E. Robb Zaring suggests:

Now before the feast of the Passover, Jesus, knowing that his hour was come that he should depart out of this world, began to be suspicious. And during supper, the devil already having put it into the heart of Judas Iscariot, Simon's son, to betray him, Jesus riseth from supper; excuseth himself; goeth out into the night; and in a little while might have been seen fleeing out of the gate through which a week before he had ridden in triumph.

He might have done the natural thing. But what he actually did at that Last Supper in the midst of the evil that he knew was closing about him was to gird himself with a towel, as the custom was, and wash his disciples' feet. He created the example of democratic helpfulness. He took in evil and he put forth good. Pure spring bubbling in the desert, the poisons filtered out and vanished, ready for any to drink of it and live!

That God should have given us this same power! What a call for men and women of dedication today! With Studdert Kennedy, I get "a pain in my mind," a lesion in my conscience, when I realize that God has given us the ability to create a better world if we want it; for if that ability is given me, it is evident that I am partly responsible for the world as it is. With uncanny clair-voyance the Negro saw himself as he really was and sang the rhythmic cadence of confession: "I was there when they crucified my Lord!" By whatever there is in me of indifference today, I was there when they crucified my Lord. I was here when they crucified America. I was part of it. In so far as I was indifferent to the possibili-ties of creating a better world and staving off *débâcle*, I drove the nails! I plunged the spear into the side of my fellow man, and now I see him on the park bench white and wasted. I gambled with the rest for his garments. There is only one way to make amends—to begin now, to dedicate myself to building a better world.

They say, Where is God in this depression? I'll tell you. He is at your elbow and mine, and saying, in a voice that may not be mistaken as he points toward the needy world: Is this nothing to you, all ye that pass by? Jesus did not pass by Jerusalem; in triumphant confidence in God, he rode into the city and began the costly building of the world which is to be. I said, *costly*.

III

JOHN ROBINSON—A COMPOSITE PICTURE
BUT A TRUE ONE

A Sermon for Those who Like a Story

*"Whosoever drinketh of the water that I shall
give him shall never thirst."*

JOHN 4:14

JOHN ROBINSON was born in the house now numbered
1470 E. 53rd Street, Chicago, when Hyde Park was still a
village. He came of a good family—his mother was a
Brown—and he and his brothers and sisters grew through
their childhood in the enjoyment of all the opportunities that good parentage and good surroundings could
give them.

It was when he was about fifteen years of age that
the experience which was to be one of the landmarks
of his life came to him. His mother had always urged him
to go to church. He had rebelled more than once, but
never from the heart. It was not that he disliked church—
it was something of a bore, to be sure, but so was school,
at times—it was only that he enjoyed reading at home
better. But because his mother and his father went regu-
larly, there was no good reason for his staying behind.

It was a Sunday in the spring of that fifteenth year of his age that he went to church as usual, but on this occasion the regular preacher was absent. His place was being taken by a youngish man who wore a Genevan gown with a stock. After the sermon began, however, John forgot the gown and stock, for the man had a simple directness about him that made him easy to listen to. The boy had the feeling, which at once pleased him and made him uncomfortable, that the minister knew all about him and was talking to him personally. He took for his text the very verse that I have chosen this morning—'Whosoever drinketh of the water that I shall give him shall never thirst."

The minister said, among other things, that the water Christ was speaking of was God's presence in a person's life. That presence was very hard to describe, but when you knew that God was God and was thinking of you, as he was thinking of all his world, the effect on you was deliciously refreshing—precisely, in fact, like the effect of drinking a sparkling glass of cold water when you were thirsty. The sun was coming in through the windows of the church while the minister described that glass of water, and it seemed to the boy, perhaps through half-shut eyes, that he could see the sunlight shimmering on a hundred glasses held by the people around him, from which they were drinking as at communion. This he knew was an illusion when he looked again, but the feeling of purity and refreshment that one has as he drinks clear water was associated in his mind afterward with the sense of the presence of God.

When, a little later, there came a chance for young people to unite with the church, and his mother proposed that he be one of them, he responded. It was the thing that every boy he knew did; his parents thought it was right to do; he entered into it as a duty not at all unpleasant, and felt he was growing up. The wine of his first communion annoyed him a little; he would have felt God's presence more clearly if he might have had a drink of clear water.

More than once during those early years he had that sense of refreshment throughout his system. Once as he looked, of a late afternoon, out over the lake from a jetty off Jackson Park, the wonder of God's creation came to him in the blue of the sky and the unbroken blue of the water before him. He drank in the infinite. Once when at night he sat in the same place and looked up at the stars, he thought of them as distant worlds, and of God great and careful enough to hold them all as a little thing in his cupped hand. He drank a refreshing draught. There was no doubt that God was God and God was good.

John had always found books attractive, and his grades at school suggested he ought to go on to college. The near-by university developing on the Midway proved a boon to him and his parents, as it did to many a Chicago family whose resources had to be husbanded for the education of more than one child.

It was not so much from the professors as from some of his fellow students that John became aware that he had been living a sheltered and even artificial existence. For one thing, there were men on the campus that used profanity he had never heard before. He learned, with no little surprise, that some of the men with good minds and fine, generous spirit had habits which he had always before associated with the blackguards and adventurers of the few novels he had read. If he could have kept up the illusion that they were a lot of fools that did not know as much about life as he did, he might have maintained his equanimity; but he began to question his own knowledge. In the classroom he came under the domination of the theory of evolution. It was all too plain: there was an unbroken chain of existence from the first forms of life through the animals to man. One might as well say it: he was himself an animal. Perhaps the men who really lived like the animals and did not care who knew it were the wise ones.

There were in him still the habits of his boyhood, which, though he was beginning to suspect them, produced in him a certain sense of oughtness. This came to him not merely as a moral but also as an æsthetic imperative. The reason he never took up cigarette-smoking, for instance, was not because he felt it was wrong. Too many men smoked whom he regarded as fine friends, to allow him to think that. He simply did not like to have a bad breath. Perhaps he never worked this out with his own reasoning powers, but it was none the less true that the thought that life ought to be beautiful counted for more with him than the thought that life ought to be good or holy.

But it was a life far emptier than it had been. He went to church on occasions still, for he liked the minister as a man. The sermons, however, simply put him on edge. He did not want to criticise, but could not help it. Some things the man said were simply not true; almost nothing was proved; and there was a lot that was said in which he had no interest whatever. There was the Bible itself. Why return to this particular channel of tradition when there was the whole past of mankind to draw from, as the university opened it up to him? And why this constant return to the idea of the supernatural? Did not everybody know that there was a natural reason for everything? Why, his own sense of having drunk the water of life, his own belief that God was near, could be easily explained on the basis of certain adolescent changes that were taking place in him at the time.

Sometimes he wished he could hold the cup to his lips once more and know that God was there, but when he tried to do so, the water was dust. He learned that there are times that you cannot find God, even when you want to.

But now I must carry you to another milestone in the career of this John Robinson. He was already out of college and studying law. He had known girls all his life. He had had his sisters to play with, and they and their friends and he and his had together led the healthy kind of group life which America had something to do with discovering. But he now found himself very much interested in individual girls. If it had not been for the demands laid upon him by his class lessons, he would have been present at some social event or other every night.

I cannot begin to tell you how he grew peculiarly conscious of Mary Lafemme. He had known her for years. They had attended the same Sunday school, the same Young People's Society. She had gone to a college in the East and had a good head on her shoulders. Her face was wise rather than beautiful. But John found himself asking if she did not have just the social command which would make her the ideal wife to match him in his career. Once after he had come home after a party where he had seen her, he wrote down on one side of a paper all the virtues he considered she had, and on the other side all her probable faults. He asked himself how she would fit into his family, and whether he could ever fit into hers. And he laughed to himself, for, though it was pleasant to remember her, he saw clearly that he did not love her—else how could he be so matter-of-fact about it all?

It was only a little later, on a fall afternoon, that he called her up and asked her to go walking with him. Happiness seemed to sweep over him like a wave when she said she would. He left his law books unopened without the shadow of a twinge of conscience. They took a train to a station thirty miles south and found themselves a country road through woodlands. They played tag with each other. They stopped, out of breath. They talked of many things. Then suddenly John realized that he had loved her for many years and that even before he had called her up he had had it planned that on this walk he was going to ask her to marry him.

I am particularly interested in one of the subjects they talked about on the way back, though everything this happy pair said to each other through that deliriously joyous afternoon was interesting enough.

John said: "I feel as if something almost supernatural has taken hold of us."

And Mary replied: "I have been feeling something like that, too. You will think me queer to mention this, but I don't think I have ever understood God before. I took in the meaning of the love of God in a rationalistic sort of way, but now it's *here*. I know he has brought us together. I know he cares. It's natural, and it's supernatural, too, for God works through nature."

But John did not think her queer to mention it. On the contrary, he wondered if anyone had ever made such an important discovery before—that love and religion are very close akin—the love of man and man, and the love of man and God.

He told Mary how he used to think that the presence of God was like water in a cup that one could drink. Now he saw that it was like the water of a *flowing* stream that poured into your arteries. It was not something that you took up, but it was like love—it took you up. It did not come to you from outside; it welled up within you. You drank of it inwardly, as it carried you on. He thought he understood at last the words of the old text, "Whosoever drinketh of the water that I give him shall never thirst. It shall be in him a well of water springing up unto everlasting life." He felt his love was eternal, and that he would never thirst again.

I must run rapidly over the years intervening between that now dim past and the present. They would take us through a war, for which John enlisted, as most of his generation did. He felt happy to do so—felt even a little disappointed that the Armistice was signed before he had been carried over to France for action. Followed ten delightful years when the little home was a-building. He and Mary moved south of Jackson Park, but not so far south that they could not enjoy a walk in it in an early summer evening. Their house was big enough for them and the children—and John's practice grew with the increasing prosperity of his city.

Look in at the most homelike scene imaginable. It is a winter night in 1928. The fire is burning on the hearth. A book or two lie on the floor in front of it, where the children, now gone to bed, have left them. John is sitting in a great chair directly in front, and Mary on the arm of it.

"We have everything," says John.

"Yes, everything," says Mary. And after a little, "I sometimes wonder if it's fair for us to have everything, when there are others who have nothing."

"Well, we can't help that," says John.

"I don't think I'm so religious as I used to be. In fact, I know I'm not. I don't feel God near me, as I used to," observes Mary, quietly.

"No," says John, honest at all costs, "we don't seem to need God the way we used to. I used to feel him carrying me on, as if I were riding a flood—do you remember that afternoon in the country?—but religion is a little stale to me now. Funny—but even life is getting a little stale. I sometimes wonder what the sense of this law business is. I sweat my head over that case for the steel mills. Why? So as to save them a few thousand dollars. So as to make a few myself. But what is the good of it? Suppose we should become the richest people in the world, would we be any happier than we are now? Sometimes life seems to me to be standing still. There is no place

(35)

for us to go, if you know what I mean. There's nothing really to do."

I met John just last week. I have come to know him quite well, though he is a bit older than I. He asked me to go to lunch with him. I could see that he had something on his mind. He has been very lucky: the depression has cost him money, but not so much as it has cost others. I made an appointment with him at a downtown club the next day.

"I don't know where to begin," he said, after we had been seated. "Perhaps it goes back to the Hombre family. My daughter waked me up about them. She has been helping in a settlement house behind the stockyards. The father is a good fellow. He has done some work for me in the garden. The son got into trouble through a drunken alderman who ran into a car he was driving, and I was asked to help him out. That's how I came to know them. The family have been on the relief list for two years or more. They exist. The kids are undernourished, but they get along. Mrs. Hombre is about to have another baby. Is that child to be welcomed into the world with gladness and singing? They talk about that child as if it were a monster: one more mouth to feed: one more body to clothe: one more weight for the family to drag through the wretchedness and hopelessness misnamed life. I tell you I get hot and wild and miserable when I think of that family and the thousands of others like them in Chicago.

"You and I are responsible for that situation. But I won't drag you into it. I'll say my profession is responsible for it. Others are responsible, too, but if we lawyers could get together we could change the face of this city. Do you know the power we have, man? Hardly an article of legislation, not any new business enterprise, and not a single court judgment but passes through our hands! Mrs. Hombre sitting on the edge of the bed, while her husband and I talk, her face white as a sheet, and worn in her late thirties as if she had lived centuries—I don't believe that's the picture God intended. I don't believe we have to endure it. If we don't like it, we can change it. I'm not going to become a professional reformer, but you can bet that I am all through thinking I'm having a wonderful time when all I'm doing is getting a little fatter in a business way. If I cannot make the money I need incidentally to making this world a decent place for humanity to live in, I'll give up making money.

"I once thought that religion was like a cup of water that you drank and it refreshed you—but it's more than that. Then I thought it was like a tide of fresh water that flowed into you. But it's more than that. I see now it's a tide of sparkling life, eternal in its meanings, which flows not merely into you but through you. The end of life is not merely to live. The old philosophers are dead right: the end of life is to live nobly and ever more nobly. It wasn't the fact of being alive that made Christ what he was; it was the cross that made him Christ. Preach on that, Padre," he said (he calls me Padre). "Tell the old Christian Church that there is still a water of life which if you drink you know you'll never feel thirsty again. But tell them it's running water, and it's high time they stopped damming it up. My God! If the Christian Church doesn't let the grace of God out into the world and lift up a new and decent social order, who will? For my part, I'm ready to go the limit. I never felt so much alive as I have since I got into this big deal— working with God to make this world a better place to live in."

IV

MARY

A Sermon for Mothers and Others

A sword shall pierce through thy own soul also that the thoughts of many hearts may be revealed.

LUKE 2:35

WHAT quality it is in her which touched the imagination of Dante, which called forth from Raphael the sweetness and mild glory of the Sistine Madonna, and which breathed the melody of the Ave into the mind of Gounod, it is difficult to tell; but in most of us, one imagines, Mary inspires an affectionate reverence because she is the eternal type of motherhood.

The Gospels give only fleeting glimpses of her life, but whenever she appears it is in the same person; in Bethlehem and Nazareth, in the temple at Jerusalem and outside Jerusalem at Golgotha, she is unchanged; she is always the mother.

"My soul doth magnify the Lord, and my spirit hath rejoiced in God, my Saviour!" Jesus was to enter the world aureoled in his mother's affection. Throughout his life this was to burn brightly upon him. Let troubles come, conspiracies snare him, or darkness gather about him, over his head the halo of his mother's love would only glow the brighter.

There was little thought of coming danger when on that night in Bethlehem Mary first saw her child, the babe in the manger. There is a beautiful legend that for her first rapt look at him the whole universe stood silent. The melodious hum of the wheeling stars was stopped; the winds of earth were hushed; the waves of ocean rested; the village noises melted into silence; the round-eyed ox and patient ass stood dumb and motionless— while Mary gazed. And as she gazed Alfred Noyes says she crooned a little song:

> Now you are mine, all mine,
> And your feet can lie in my hand so small,
> And your tiny hands in my heart can twine,
> And you cannot walk, so you never shall fall
> And be pierced by the thorns beside the door
> Or the nails that lie upon Joseph's floor;
> Through sun and rain, through shadow and shine,
> You are mine, all mine ——[1]

A song of love.

But motherhood means more than love. When Mary and Joseph presented the child at the temple for the rite of purification forty days after his birth, they were met by the saintly patriarch, Simeon. Perceiving the hope of

[1] Reprinted by permission from "Slumber Songs of the Madonna" in *Collected Poems*, Vol. I, by Alfred Noyes. Copyright, 1908, by Frederick A. Stokes Company.

Israel in the child, the aged man took him in his arms and prayed, "Lord, now lettest thou thy servant depart in peace, according to thy word, for mine eyes have seen thy salvation"; and turning to Mary he said, "Behold this child is set for the fall and rising again of many in Israel —yea, a sword shall pierce through thy own soul also." Her fancy can hardly then have anticipated the full prophetic import of the utterance, but a few years were to open to her the truth that motherhood, meaning love, must mean also a sword in the soul.

"Son, why hast thou thus dealt with us? Behold thy father and I have sought thee sorrowing." Mary's first recorded words to her son come from a soul the sword's edge has already touched. Jesus, at the age of twelve, had left his parents in order to talk with people of the outside world. Mary was beginning to learn the meaning of full motherhood. He and she were not one will, but two. In the boy whose flesh had once been hers she saw the unfolding of a soul which was not hers, but his own— his own unsharable soul. It is the inevitable price of in- dividuality. A widening gulf separated them which would impair her power of protecting him. The breach would have brought no anxiety to her, if only she had not loved him; but this is love's peculiar torment, that, if it be not detestable self-love, it must be parted from the object of its care. And if parted, then lacking power completely to enfold and to defend. A father once whis- pered to his children:

"I have you fast in my fortress
And will not let you depart. . . ."

But this is only a poet's fancy. He could retain the
thought of them in his mind, but as for themselves, they
were to be their own free spirits, grave Alice and laughing Allegra and Edith with golden hair, each meeting
life beyond parental tutelage, single-handed. Human
motherhood is love which desires, but cannot forever
defend, its children.

Only a handful of years and Jesus is a man grown,
his preaching of the Word on the shore of Galilee, his
training of the twelve, his last week's mission in the capi-
tal, completed. Now he waits in Gethsemane. Mary is
not there; but it does not exaggerate motherhood to
imagine her, now with whitened hair, sitting in her room
at the inn, or at the house of a friend in Jerusalem, whither
she has come for the feast, and thinking of that little child
of more than thirty years before.

On the next day, when she enters the city—she comes
upon a crowd about a public building. She has heard
nothing of what has happened in the night. Possibly these
people have gathered to hear words of life from the lips
of her son again, as in the past! Her Jesus may be preaching to them—from the prophets, say—from one of the
giant texts of Isaiah. Finally she sees him in the midst
of them. God have mercy! He *is* preaching to them,
from the text: "He was wounded for our transgressions,
he was bruised for our iniquities, the chastisement of our

peace was upon him, and with his stripes we are healed."
He it is, lashed to the pillar. Upon him falls the rod of
the soldier. What was Mary to do?—every stripe in his
flesh was a gash in her heart. How much easier to have
died for him than to look! But it is not given that
mothers should always stand between their sons and
circumstances.

The cross was heavy on the shoulder of Jesus as they
drove him out past the city wall. And when at last the
abominable thing was placed, of what did watching Mary
think? She could remember sunny Galilee; she could re-
call that yesterday when the boy played with the other
boys at Nazareth; but did not the darkness and the silence
take her back to the stable of Bethlehem? And within
her did there not well up in anguish the heart-breaking
minor of that cradle song?

Now you are mine, all mine. . . .

(And Christ on his cross!)

This is the irony of motherhood, a love that cares
for but cannot finally take care of its own.

Evidently there is a strain of motherhood in each one
of us. Have you never endured the moment when you
would have gone to a rescue but could not?

Perhaps it was your child who was taken with a
mounting fever, and you waited all night by the bed-
side. You listened to the ticking clock and the beating

heart beside you and wondered if one should lag and drop out of the race before morning. But you could do nothing.

Perhaps it is a loved one who is far away, and between him and you are sea dangers or city dangers or dangers of the highroad. What can you do? Nothing.

Or it is your social order, which you dream of making Christian. An old woman, representing the uncounted poor, asks you for a penny in your doorway, her bent back telling its tale of unending labor, the lines of sadness on her face indelible and deep. You ask her a few questions: *Where did you come from?* She names the county whence she had been brought as a child. In your fancy's eye you see her, a little curly-haired thing in the arms of her mother as they appeared at the door of a friend's house to spend the first night in the city of their hope. *How old are you?* She knows she is over sixty, though not exactly how much. You see the operation of that law whereby, when experience becomes too bitter to be borne, consciousness dulls off into callousness and we forget. *Married?* That is a long story, for she has been married not once, but many times: but now for some time she has been alone. You see her as a young girl, clothed with such attractions of feature and dress as she has been able to wrest from the slum, coming with her man to the rectory to be married; then the beginning of her long battle, lost before it was started, to keep love alive and the home intact in face of penury and alcohol and the steely hardness of her environment; then the leaving that husband; and after a little, because she was desperate in her loneliness, finding another, with fewer hopes to be extinguished this time, but with disillusionment as certain as death, none the less; and so on, moving often, as evictions threatened; all the once virtues of her character ebbing away in the wake of self-respect, until now there is nothing left but the animal residuum of hunger and the instinct of self-preservation. *Any children?* She has had children. She has seen four of them die. She thinks three are still alive, but God knows where they are. You can see the back rooms in which the children grew up, the first welcomed and much loved, the second less loved, following so close that the mother's arms were hardly rested from the first; then the third, unless the merciful agony of a miscarriage should have intervened; and for those who live, a childhood on the filthy streets; the meretricious ideals that children acquire who are suckled on the spirit of the street gang; the pitiable non-resistance of the children to the sinister forces that presently sweep in, catch their youth, dissolve their morals, and make them, like their mother, anonymous flotsam on the social tides of the great city.

Go to *their* rescue! Change *that* social order! See that tomorrow there are no more such old women begging bread. But the forces of evil have the start upon you by generations: you will not stay their momentum in your lifetime: and at the last you may remember Mary, who saw the Jesus whom she loved crucified—and could not save him.

But come now! Have we seen the last picture of Mary? Did she leave the scene at Calvary a broken woman? Did she sullenly curse God for his inexorableness and cruelty? Nothing could be farther from the fact. Only a few weeks later we find her in exultant prayer!

Mary's problem, after the crucifixion, was how to face her loss. She had the insight to see that the only way to view it was from the standpoint of eternity. She knew that the question she needed to have answered was one to be asked at the end of time: will my love for Jesus prove finally to have been in vain, or will it not? He has now been murdered. Is this a symbol of what the universe does to all its children in the end? Is our separation forever? Or is there something more than murder at the heart of things? Will the last eternal scene justify my love?

She had to choose. She knew there was no compromise; she realized the truth that poets, teachers, moralists, and prophets have all labored to make known, that life at bottom is a tremendous either-or. Either thou wilt believe that love will be justified or thou wilt believe that it will not. Thou canst not believe both. Thou canst not believe neither. To attempt to believe neither is to believe that it will not.

But more, had Mary been of a philosophical turn of mind, she might have come in her deeper moments to know there is a changeless preference hidden in the two apparent alternatives: belief in the justification of love is positive; it accords with the basic positiveness of reality. Despair is negation; it belongs to non-reality. Fundamental doubt applied to itself calls for fundamental doubting of itself, but fundamental belief applied to itself only confirms its own fundamental nature. It is a more realistic response to life to face it with the trinity of faith, hope, and love than not to do so. It is the way of the hero to dare to love greatly; it is the coward who has no cause; and no severest fit of doubt, wherein all other truths may seem to be awash and foundering, can quite disturb the sureness of the fact that heroism is always, always, always, preferable to cowardice.

Mary can hardly have indulged in these general reflections. The truth, we may imagine, must have come to her more personally as instinctive knowledge, woven into the fabric of her own relationship to Christ. Would she believe her love for him would finally be proved to have been vain? Never would she believe that, and for this one reason: she would have deeply felt that *such a belief was disloyal to her love for him*. If her love for him was real, then it was real eternally. To have believed that in the long last her love for him would be proved to have had no meaning would have made her love a shadow of itself. She could not at once believe that and love him as she did. Complete love demanded a complete belief.

Whether or not Mary gave herself to reflection, here at least is the starting-point for philosophy and religion. Those who have dared to love heroically and unselfishly know a secret that is hidden from others; the world is made for them. For them alone it has an ultimate meaning. They feel at home in it, and no wonder; they are its most understanding children. They know their own love reflects the love of the Ruler of it. They eagerly look forward to the day when all things shall be seen in the light of eternity, for they know that God, being God, will at last express his own love in absolute entirety; nothing will be lacking; all that is holy in your loves and mine will be rewarded; their eternal meaning will stand clear.

Such is, doubtless, the inner truth of the tradition of the ancient church, that the grave never held Mary. Her only reward can have been reunion with her son. When her days were done, it is said, the angels, ministering to her, took her, clothed in life eternal, to Jesus, in the highest heaven. Human speech and conception cannot measure the fullness of her glory there. The magnificence of the sky at sunset, the radiance of Ezekiel's vision of the sapphire throne on the cloud of fire, these and other sublimities of sight and fancy all fall short. Mary now reigns, the queen of heaven, joy of saints and angels.

The way of motherhood to many may seem tragic (to care, and not be able to protect!), but we survey the events only between birth and death, while God has all eternity to show his meanings and his issues. That God should have made the instinct of heroic love the deepest passion of all noble souls tells all we need to know about his character and his eventual purpose. There comes, in God's eternity, a day of gladness, a day of victory, an unfading day, for those who, in spite of all its costs, have allowed themselves the experience of such selfless love as filled the heart of Mary.

If you do not know this to be true, you had better look no longer at humanity, its poverty, disease, and ignorance. The sight can only be discouraging. It will only tear your hopes to tatters and leave nothing in their place. Your very knowledge will make you pessimistic, for you will know the universe is vaster than humanity and you together: it has more power: its word, and not yours, will be the last: its will shall finally be done. Best turn your eyes aside. Best stand aside, for you are not instrumented for the work of history: you are not equipped redemptively: you have not wherewith to supply mankind with the first essential, faith.

But if you know the universe is only the minister of God, your Father, and that God's love must one day make prevail all of your love that accords with his; if you know that in a just cause for which men have given all they had and seemingly in vain, the failures are only battles lost in a war not lost nor to be lost; if you are aware that humanity, when it escapes your care, falls not into stark cosmic neglect but into the hands of God; then you are armed for the warfare of reality. Then we need you! Then we desperately need you. Come in and help us! You stand with Mary. Stand with us: before all other things we need your faith!

V

THE LAST REFUGE OF A SCOUNDREL

A Sermon for Patriots

"And I John saw the holy city, new Jerusalem, coming down from God out of heaven."
REV. 21:2

THUS the prophet pictured in his dream the coming of a better world. Living not in a world of nations, as we do, but in a world in which cities dominated the scene, he dreamed of a coming city of cities. Being a Jew, he called the city the New Jerusalem. Had he lived today, he would doubtless have had in mind a nation of nations, and had he not been a Jew he might have sought for some broader name than Jerusalem. Perhaps he would have said, "I, John, saw the holy nation, the new humanity, coming down from God out of heaven."

One feels drawn to this prophet—for who is it that some time or other has not dreamed about the world as it might be, the world as God would have it, the world of a better humanity? It is usually given to young people to dream graciously about the future, but we who are older have not outgrown a certain kind of dreaming;

(51)

and it seems fitting that I should unburden myself now of a plan for making a better world which may commend itself to the dream of all of you.

Beginning with the presupposition that the most serious problem facing human society today is the international problem—for it is the vastest; it is biggest with possibility for weal or woe; it is the most inclusive— we have first to discover what it is that allows of discord between the nations and leads at times to war. The answer is the quintessence of logic; the occasion of war is the disunity that subsists between nations. They are separated from one another by rifts of mutual misunderstanding, bad feeling, mistaken purpose—and through these rifts peers the grisly face of Mars. To substitute unity for disunity is then the basis of our plan for bringing in the kingdom of heaven.

1. Since one of the most obvious reasons for mutual misunderstanding is the *multiplicity of languages and other expressions of our various cultures*, it would doubtless be profitable to work toward unity in this field. The reproof hidden in Philip Guedalla's delicious paragraph may be taken to heart by others besides Britons:

To the Englishman his island is a piece of land entirely surrounded by foreigners. The majority of these people are believed to live in a continent lying off the mouth of the Thames and known as Europe. Certain parts of it, as, for example, the Swiss mountains, the French Riviera, and the Italian picture galleries, are reserved for the holidays of Englishmen; but the remainder is entirely given up to foreigners. These foreigners, it has been observed by Englishmen who have ventured among them, differ in degree but not in kind. They are marked in every instance by an obstinate refusal to converse in English. This unreasonable objection compels the Englishman to toy lightly (or painfully) with the various absurd languages which they use among themselves.— (*Supers and Supermen* p. 66.)

And foreignness involves more than mere difference in language: the roots of reciprocal distrust between nations penetrate to all those manners and customs which differentiate one civilization from another.

The solution immediately suggests itself: the nations of the world would do better if they all spoke the same language and enjoyed the same culture—and since the English language is the most widely spoken, and Anglo-American civilization the widest flung, the quickest way to secure peace through understanding would seem to be to bring the entire world within the circle of our own culture.

2. *Diversity in sentiment* plays no little part in permitting international evils to develop. Even if we all spoke the same language and used the same cultural symbols in general, the feeling toward those symbols would still be different in the several nations. What the American tourist calls dirt on Italian buildings the Florentine artist calls color. What is religion to one person is Antichrist to another.

Differences of faith seem absurd to those outside the emotional limits wherein they arise—Carlyle grunts his scorn of the diphthong that separates the great Eastern from the great Western Church—but they are none the less facts to be reckoned with. Whether the critics will or no, a cross attracts a Christian by its memory of sacrifice; it repels a Jew, since for him it stands for centuries of repression in the sunless ghetto, for the Christians who in the Middle Ages coming from church pulled the beards of the Jews they met, for massacre in Poland, for boycott in Germany.

There seems to be one clear way out of this diversity of sentiment. We should begin early, and teach all our children the same attitudes—and since religion is the great treasure house of sentiment, we should adopt all of us the same religion. It is quite clear that that religion should not be Buddhism or Confucianism or Mohammedanism, for they still carry the taint of heathenism. It would be some form of Christianity; but Eastern Christianity is eliminated because it is Eastern, and Catholicism, because of its obvious shortcomings—and that leaves Protestantism as the world religion. The argument is skillfully summed up in the dictum of Goldsmith's Parson Thwackum: "When I say religion, I mean the Christian religion, and when I say the Christian religion, I mean the Protestant religion!"

3. If you will allow me to pursue this satirical vein one more period, I will point out the way to resolve the world's *disunity of purpose*. This nation has a manifest destiny: this is proved by the words of generations of Fourth of July orators. "More automobiles are used in

our Flint County, Michigan, alone, than in the whole of France"; "our New York City has reared the highest structure ever raised by the hand of man"; "our nation as a whole chews more gum than all the jaws of Europe could have held a thousand years ago";—and many more such pearls might be added to our diadem. It might be said, besides, that we are an essentially peaceful people. Since this is the case, is it not as vivid as the colors at the World's Fair that peace can best be won if American industry gradually broadens until it encompasses the whole earth, if the dollar becomes the recognized base of exchange, and if in general the purposes of all the world are unified about the vast benign purpose of American expansion?

You smile at this 100 per cent Nordic Protestant American hope for the race, for impracticability protrudes from it as generously as needles from a porcupine. What is there about the English language and Anglo-American culture that makes it superior to the French, for instance? The language is doubtless better for British and Americans, for they are brought up on it (and one would hate to have to put in any more hours on French irregular verbs); but go to such a country as Egypt, where the two cultures are locked in struggle for the supremacy, and there exhibit evidence that would convince all that the Anglo-Saxon is the superior language and culture! What is there in the commercial enterprise of America that makes its success more advantageous to the world at large than that of Germany or Italy? We are lovers of peace, we protest: but so are they: no commercial people with their eyes in their head today believe that war is anything but a disrupting and wasteful method of adjusting international disputes. I have never heard that the merchants of Sao Paulo, Montevideo, and the other ports of South America make traders from Chicago more welcome than those from Geneva or Hamburg simply because these can argue that they came from Chicago. And as for Protestantism being the universal religion—we shall come to that.

The point to be noted here is that the way of building toward the future which I have been describing, for all its impracticability from the viewpoint of peace, is the *natural* one. *It is the kind in which we are all engaged*. We are proud of the culture of our city and invite the people of all nations to come to it. We believe in our church and our denominations, sending our missionaries to the farthest quarters of the globe to give the black man and the brown the interpretations of life which have meant so infinitely much to us. And at this moment our emissaries are in Geneva to do all that in them lies to make the world safe for American commerce. It is natural that the nation should grow, and seek to grow, in this wise—organically—like a plant—like a living creature.

We could abide this if it were only the natural way,

but according to its results it is the consummately *dangerous* way. Mere organic growth is the occasion of the struggle for existence and the unspeakable mortality among creatures of the jungles; and so it is also among men and notions. The rivalry of expanding cultures was the cause of many, if not most, of the early wars of the world; the rivalry of growing religions was the cause of the desperate military venture of the Crusades, as of the bloodshed and famine of the Hundred Years' War; and the rivalry of increasing economic powers is the key to almost every modern war. Promoting our own nation with a cavalier disregard of others is not only not the way to peace, but because other nations are doing the same thing, it is the one perfect preparation for war. Because a thousand firms in Germany and an equal thousand in England were going it blind, contesting the field for markets, military war came riding in upon the back of their commercial war—and many more than a thousand young men presently felt the little sting of machine-gun bullets, or the flesh-tearing shrapnel, fell forward, spat a little blood (if they had a face left to spit it from), and died. And if the same national forces are left abroad and unbridled in the world today, do you think the laws of sociology will be escaped? Do you fondly believe that your son's or your nephew's or your own brow will be able to resist the kiss of the bullet, or your brain or theirs deny it its bed? War is death; and

unconditioned national growth is war. As it was yesterday, so must it be tomorrow.

But we have almost forgotten our text. John did not
say that he saw the holy city, the holy nation, the new
humanity growing like a plant from a particular spot—
from an American or a British or any other base. He
was aware of the deceitfulness of the whole philosophy
of morals which holds that most important to a man is,
first, himself, then his family, then his city, then his
nation, and then humanity. He knew that the loyalty
growing from so mean a base could not possibly bear
the fruit of future good.

He saw the new humanity descending from heaven. You
who have flown know the viewpoint one enjoys descending from heaven. It is not the small that one sees first as
he looks down from the height, but the large. The whole
landscape stretches out under him, an immense disc. As
he nears the earth, the larger features of the country become visible, the rivers and highroads; then the lesser,
the farms and the landing-field. Finally, the buildings and
runways of the landing-field itself catch and hold the
attention. The landing-field, indeed, could not have been
found directly had not the pilot gauged its position, before he could actually distinguish it, from his view of
the entire country beneath him.

It is well known that a change comes over a person
when he begins to follow in the way of Christ and take

God in earnest. One of the features of that change is that his point of reference changes: he turns from seeing the large in the light of the small to seeing the small in the light of the large. He begins to have *the viewpoint of one coming down from heaven*. He strives to see the world as God sees it. He ceases to see himself as the center of importance in life, his other relationships lying about him in concentric circles which decrease in importance as the distance from him increases; he is no longer one of those who stand on their own base and proceed to spread root and branch over all the immediate neighborhood—as the nations have done. To him the most important matter has become humanity; once he knows how humanity lies, he can fix the ideal position for his own nation; once he knows the needs of his nation, he can tell how to educate his family; once he knows the educational requirements of his family, he knows how to make his own adjustments. He has become a member of the brotherhood-to-be coming down from heaven.

Now at last we have a way of substituting unity for disunity which does not contradict and destroy itself. The unity of the brotherhood-to-be, the unity of the Kingdom of Heaven, is not arrived at by the domination of any part over the whole—a dominion rightly subject to dispute by any other part. It is the unity which takes the whole for granted, and to that whole demands the adjustment of each part. It works from the world to the nations; the oneness of God's world is the first fact of existence to those who know him.

So you may choose which kind of patriot to be. You may be the kind who believes in his country first and then in humanity, if possible. You will be impatient at the innumerable international conferences continually being held. You will write impassioned letters to the newspapers begging that our delegates pack their bags and come home because they cannot have their way. You will add yours to the sinister influence of that part of the press which is the evil genius of our country. One can hardly say with Dr. Johnson that that patriotism is the last refuge of a scoundrel, for often, as we have pointed out, it is a natural unthought-out patriotism, having no regard to consequences. Call it, therefore, rather the last refuge of a blind man.

But on some of you the light has dawned! You are pro-human before you are pro-American. It is because you are pro-human that you are pro-American. You will be useful at and in support of all international conferences because your first concern will be to devise means just for all alike, and therefore beneficial to your own country. You will be a patriot of a most desirable kind because your patriotism will derive from a concern for the general good in which your own country can increasingly prosper: it will not issue in a vertigo of rivalries and finally in the bloody holocaust of war. The world calls for the leadership of you who will belong to the company viewing life "coming down out of heaven."

If this be the message of Protestantism, then Protestantism is the universal religion.

VI

GIVE ME A MAN

A Sermon for Young People

"Choose you a man!"
I Sam. 17:8

Do you remember who said that? It was Goliath, the giant, the ogre of your childhood. It was when the children of Israel were waging one of their frequent wars with the Philistines and were camped on one side of a valley, with the enemy opposite, that this big swaggerer, nine feet tall, with half a ton of armor on him (according to the report of his opponents), walked up and down outside the Israelites' lines and defied them: "Give me a man, that we may fight together: choose you a man for you, and let him come down to me." And the story runs that in the camp of Israel there was found only one man to accept the challenge—a man with the appearance of a child, the stripling, David—though there were many children there with the appearance of men. The whole heroic tale is told in the seventeenth chapter of I Samuel.

Heroic tales such as this—tales of Odysseus, of Æneas,

of Siegfried, of Roland—seem all to belong to the distant past. But this is not strictly true. There is an inveterate element of adventure in everyday living. You have, in fact, only to rename the participants to appreciate how very up-to-date the Goliath story is.

Nothing is more certain, for instance, in this day when the knowledge of the human mind has so greatly increased, that you and I, though individuals, are many individuals in one. Every person has his business—is a manufacturer, salesman, transportation expert, housekeeper, or the like—but if that were his only character he would become a mere robot (as many people do). He has his hobbies, recreations: he is a golfer, collector of first editions, rose-grower, and he is likely to have still other genuine interests to which, since his day has in it only twenty-four hours, he can devote no time at all. His unexpressed wishes may show him to be a literary man, an educator, an artist. It is certain that everyone is part theologian—for we all have our ideas of God—and part statesman—for we all have a political penchant. In a word, you are not better described as a man than as an army of men. For the moment I will call you an Israelitish army.

You are encamped there, behind your brow, perfectly defended—at least so far as any of the rest of us can see, for God hath so wrought that no man's individuality may be penetrated without his own consent. From the outside we cannot tell what thoughts are moving singly, or in squad or company formations, through your camp, what affections are marshaling them, what motives are preparing them for a sally. You are yourself; you are your own army. No one will entice you into the valley from your hill fastness unless you desire it yourself. And that, apparently, is also the position in which the Israelites found themselves.

But life does not leave you alone. In some form or other it goes stalking up and down outside, challenging, "Come on out and fight!" And it puts your army within in a flutter. What shall I send out to take up this challenge? you ask yourself. You may be asking yourself that question this very morning if you are a young man or woman trying to hit upon a life-occupation. Shall I send me out a well-trained clerk, a lawyer, a buyer, or what? Which one will best stand up against that challenger and force the fighting into his own territory?

But life, calling from outside, does not seem particular about what kind of profession your defense may assume. It seems particular, like Goliath of old, about one thing only: "Give me a *man*, that we may fight together: choose you a *man* for you, and let *him* come down to me." Mature strength and wisdom is what life demands. Half a man will not do—neither will half a woman.

Choose you a *man*.

One great part of our difficulties with life comes of our failing to choose our best selves for our experiences. We send into life our next-best, immature, childish selves.

We do not choose a man for our battle; we choose a child.

Anyone may make his own list of the childish characters in which we allow ourselves to appear. I take mine largely from Professor Overstreet.

We expect children to boast, for instance, "I've got an uncle who is as rich as any man in the world." "My father could lick any man on the block." "My mother's almost a hundred years old!" Sometimes the suggestions are rather overpowering! They are all very well in children; but in a man, how puerile! Yet there is many a man who in his physical maturity still continues to rely on boasting to maintain himself as he faces the world: "You can't tell me anything about life." "My country could lick any country on earth." "This is the world's greatest newspaper." Pure childishness! Isolated individual acquaintances of that type are not, however, so disquieting a phenomenon, for they may be quickly assigned to their place. A more significant circumstance is that a great part of the public seems to demand that type of person for a leader. What we dislike among our friends we regard as natural and even necessary in public men. Even when we have learned not to boast ourselves, our choice of party standard-bearers still reveals our want of maturity. On the whole, we do not vote for political candidates who do not rave about their records, their party, and what they'll do when elected, in superlatives. We usually send children to vote for us.

Akin to the child-man who boasts is the child-man who bullies. It has been said that bullying is boasting with one's fists, or whatever substitutes for fists can be found. "Bullying, whatever form it takes, is an effort to gain power not by intelligently meeting the demands of the situation—coöperating with the other person, trying to understand him, realizing his rights and his possibilities, but by violently dominating the situation." If a child cannot hold his place among children his own physical size, he is likely to make up for this loss by making children smaller than he is fear him. But in a man! We have seen it sometimes in a foreman, who, fearing he may lose his own position, takes his fears out on the man under him. We have seen it in an executive who, waited upon by representatives of his labor, dismisses them without a hearing with a gruff, "I don't need anybody else to run my business for me." It is in evidence in the military officer whose specialties are profanity and punishment. He was well drawn as Himmelstoss in *All Quiet on the Western Front*. It is always in a little person trying to be recognized as big. Instead of being big, in a man's way, by achieving large sympathies and an understanding mind, he tries to be big in a child's way—by using threats and force over those whom chance has placed in his power.

Perhaps we are not so apt to send, to live for us, a child who boasts and bullies, as a child with tantrums. We know the child who throws himself down on the sidewalk and kicks and shouts, "I hate you, I hate you, I hate you," until he gets what he has been begging for. He has learned by an instinct which to our fathers was sure proof of original sin that you are likely to let him have anything he wants rather than endure a public scene. The child will grow out of this if he has wise parents, but there is less hope for the tantric (I believe the adjective is as permissible as the noun) adult. We know him, too. He is one who presents himself to life as a child, hoping for—and sometimes getting—what he wants in the way of a child. It is sometimes amusing to hear a taxi-driver in a foreign city tell another driver who disputes a crossing with him what he considers the situation calls for. The whole block becomes acquainted with the one driver's opinion of the other—and of the other's ancestors on both his father's and his mother's side. Not so amusing is it when the tantrum happens to be the favorite indoor sport of your husband: "When are we ever going to have supper!" "This soup is like dishwater!" "Will those children ever be quiet!" or of the wife: "This is a pretty time to come to supper!" "The soup won't stay hot forever!" "If *you* had the children!" We live like little people when we do not employ the calm and balanced mind of an adult.

But the most colossal type of infantilism in America is yet to be mentioned. In infancy and very early childhood, before the mental controls are built up, complete unrestraint seems the one thing worth living for. Oh, to be able to play any time we wanted to, and anywhere—even after supper and on the neighbor's lawn! Oh, for excitement—all the fires we wanted to build, all the guns we wanted to shoot! Oh, for enough candy to eat; they have taken two and a half tons of it on the expedition to the South Pole—gee, I wisht I was Commander Byrd! Oh, for staying up late—I'd never go to bed if I had my way! Children beyond the pale of parental guidance do often overindulge themselves, as many green apple orchards might testify. The normal child finally brings himself up to disciplined living. But some children, though they assume the features of manhood and womanhood, do not really grow up. They will have their way. They will obey just as few moral or civic laws as possible. In business they become the champions of that Rugged Individualism which is nothing but Rugged Selfishness and leads to the sweatshop and child labor. In society they become those people who want all and give nothing. They live chiefly for pleasure, as a child does. Dancing and drinking are their rocking-horse and candy—and jazz their rattle. The character they send out against life is a child's; and the rewards which come from noble living are denied them.

But life says: "Choose you a *man*, that we may fight together." And it is certain that we shall never conquer unless we do. Ah, but how to do it! How! If only the past could come true again in us, if only we might find the man, the David—our noblest self—to do battle for us! Professor Gossip has finely spoken of the Hero in Thy Soul, but where is he? The everyday life we have to live does not conduce to heroism.

The fact is that instead of encouraging the David within us we tend to do exactly what was done in the camp of the Israelites: when he begins to make himself known we are likely to snub and belittle him.

Eliab was one of the army—one of those who should have taken up the challenge of Goliath but was not man enough to do so. Perhaps it is natural that, belonging to the mediocrity himself, he did not like to see David going ahead. According to the Scripture, "Eliab's anger was kindled against David and he said, Why camest thou down hither? I know thy pride, and the naughtiness of thine heart!" David had not only Goliath to struggle against; he had his own fellow soldiers.

Why is it that human society continually persecutes those who are different from the average? Always we stone our prophets. Lavoisier, perhaps the greatest chemist and certainly one of the greatest men France ever produced, was haled from his house by a mob and condemned by a judge who, in pronouncing sentence, declared, "The Republic has no need of chemists." Rembrandt, when his masterpiece, "The Night Watch," was displayed, was so viciously attacked by his fellow artists and the critics who did not like his new technique, that orders ceased to come and he was reduced to a poverty from which he never emerged. Marco Polo, one of the most interesting and certainly the most truthful of medieval travelers, was greeted, on his return to Italy from China, by a storm of abuse and derision which has affected his reputation to this day. Who could believe stories about paper money and books printed by a machine and black stones that burned like wood? So David himself was disparaged by the army he belonged to.

The same situation seems usually to prevail in the inner army of a person's mind. The childish elements fear to let the man among them step forth. The man in you may not be a Lavoisier, but he is certainly a chemist. God intended you to be the kind of chemist that David became—a chemist of life. He designed you, as he designed all of his heroes, to study and know the imponderable elements of existence, to reject those that destroy, and to fuse those that build into creative and enthusiastic life service. But you are likely, if you are not on the watch, to crowd this outstanding man under and give the control of your career to the second-best forces that shut you out from heroic combat. The man in you may not be a Rembrandt, but he is certainly an artist—in living. You may not, however, give that artist a chance. The childish business of being like the Joneses next door may rob you of your individual destiny. The picture you paint may be only a caricature of your real possibilities; if it is only your second-rate self who does your living for you, your life will inevitably lose color and perspective.

Again, the man in you may not be a Marco Polo—but what a traveler he might be! Don't you know that we are hungering for what you may bring us back from the land of the ideal? There is a country farther than Cathay, more romantic than the India of Polo, "an older place than Eden, and a taller town than Rome," whose language is the laughter of little children, whose coinage is the sterling worth of a man's word, whose armies are the empowering intimations of immortality, whose government is the unescapable fact of God. Let David the traveler stand forth and tell us of *that* country! But, no, you are more likely, if you are like the rest of us, to repress that traveler and content yourself with the comfortable and unadventurous, the vegetative and stay-at-home virtues of the middling man in the middling community. Things as they are are good enough for us (as if they were!); we won't worry our heads about things as they might be and should be. Go on back, David. Why camest thou down hither?—retire to forgetfulness: the children of the army will have their way.

Wait. The hero is there in that camp of yours, and if you would like to bring him out, there is still a way to do so. The finding of the man in your soul is one of the glorious capacities of the Gospel.

Of course the distinction between childishness and childlikeness is well understood. Childishness, which is a form of littleness, is never tolerable: childlikeness, an ex-

(71)

pansive trait, is a quality which sometimes expresses itself even in the very great. All healthy adults find pleasure in times of recreation by being childlike again—by playing bear on the floor with the little children of the family, throwing themselves into the excitement of a football game, or laughing when the custard pies in the movies speed to their mark—it is part of the rhythm of life in times of relaxation to go back to childhood, but we have our estimate of a man who never grows out of childhood. How will even the Gospel avail to bring the childish to send a man to represent them in life?

It is all quite simple. People are children because their world is small, as a child's is small; and no man is ever larger than his world. The things of the small world are supremely important because they are, to him, the only things that are. It is because little Jack lives in a world consisting only of things to play with and things to eat that they mean so much to him; the rest of the world has no meaning whatever. When, therefore, he wants that ball, he wants it. No use to tell him there will be a long day tomorrow when he can play with it to his heart's content. No use to tell him you know another little boy in Oak Park who never cries for his ball (which probably is not true, anyway). No use to tell him he is not being fair to his nurse by splitting the welkin and her eardrums with his shouts. Tomorrow, the boy in Oak Park, fairness—these are part of a man's world, and would make it easy for a man to forego having the ball: but they are not part of the boy's world. The ball, however, is, and that he will have.

Similarly, when we possess childish characters, our world is constricted. It is reduced to the interests of food, shelter, sex, and social position—that is, to the sole interests of a minimum man. We must maintain our place at home or in business or elsewhere, and we'll do it by boasting or bullying or in some other childish way, if we have to. No use, then, to tell us that from the broad viewpoint of eternity it is better to be right than president. No use, then, to tell us that if we will only consent to live humbly we shall enjoy deeper insights into life. No use, then, to tell us that the lovely things of this world are all born of sorrow. These matters of the good, the true, and the beautiful are not part of our world; and our little selfish spot in the puddle *is*.

The one thing needful is to live in a big world. A man is a man because he lives in a man's world. If you would be saved from being the boaster or bully, the easily angered, the insatiable self-seeker, if you would encourage and not deny the David in your mental army, live in a larger world.

How? By letting the Gospel touch you. You find yourself then in an eternal place. You have a work to do in history assigned you by the One who presides over all history. All objects fall into their proper perspective. Food, shelter, sex, and social position are seen in their right dimensions when we look to God and his timeless purpose; they are seen to be the means through which the majestic ends of life are reached. You will not be guilty of the childish error of mistaking what to live *with* for what to live *for*. You will do your day's work as part of the great work of the coming kingdom. A maturity will come on, which, like David's, will not be lacking in youthfulness; for all those are youthful who know there is a future. We are here to work, as ability is given us, the works of a liberally just, supremely benevolent Father, who inhabits eternity. Those who know this enjoy a poise that is not given to others. They do not cry and pant after the little material toys and physical indulgences: they know the joys of a larger world. If you live only in a little house on Main Street, you will grow old sighing for the transitory pleasures of Main Street. If you have in you the mind of Christ and think in terms of humanity and the long aims of God, the little things of life will not baffle you. You will rejoice to be able to respond adequately to the challenge, "Give me a man!"

VII

GETTING ON, GETTING HONOR, GETTING HONEST

A Sermon for People of Insight

"Moses, whom the Lord knew face to face . . ."
Deut. 34:10

But the Lord did not know him face to face in the early years of his life. Moses did not then turn his face to the Lord, so that he might be known. Through the years before he came to maturity we find him in various places —fleeing for his life from the land of Egypt after he had killed the Egyptian, marrying Zipporah, the daughter of the high priest of Midian, working for his father-in-law by tending the flocks—but everywhere being carried along by his own ambitions, a devotee (to use the phrase of George Bernard Shaw) of the Gospel of Getting On. That his chief interest was largely himself finds additional proof in the series of excuses he presented to the Lord when at the burning bush he was commanded to give up the business of tending flocks and go back to his own unhappy people under the scorching Egyptian sun.

If we take the popular saying, *getting on, getting*

honor, getting honest, to represent the three degrees of living, Moses was moving along on the first, simple, *positive* level—the level on which most of us pursue our careers. We feel that it is quite necessary to get on.

One's standard, at this level, is one's own desires. They are the goads of getting on, and they are the goals. One's very instincts keep him on the way. A modern novel by an author of a somewhat cynical turn of mind describes the conversation between an old man and a younger one as they stand on a hill just at the edge of a city of the Old World and look down on the human life below them. The younger man makes the obvious comparison and sees men and women like ants in a great anthill. The older man thinks ants are too mild and kindly, that ants are not selfish enough to be compared with men. But both agree that the population is driven for the most part by the instincts for food, warmth, power, and the rest. "Men have got to live."

"But men have *not* got to live," is the reply of all heroic souls since the race began. Emerson said that life was worth only so much and that the toleration, for instance, of the evil of slavery was too high a price to pay for it. The human family has actually gone from strength to strength because there have been some members of it willing to die for the common good. Sometimes getting on comes into conflict with the second *comparative* degree of living, getting honor; and then there is only one course open to the brave. The call of honor, the call of the high standards of your society, holds the call of getting on in abeyance.

Moses reached this pitch at the burning bush. In spite of his first selfish demurral, the record stands that he finally rose to the point of honor and took up the burden of his people. He knew that the great longing of the Hebrew heart was for freedom, and to that freedom he devoted himself without reserve. In behalf of his people he stood before the Pharaoh, and for his people's weal he led them across the wind-swept Red Sea inlet and on from oasis to oasis in the Midian desert; for them he climbed the dreadful slope of Sinai, where dwelt the God Jehovah in the midst of lightnings. He began to live the life of an honorable leader among them, making his own ambition secondary to their welfare.

In the philosophy of science called "emergent evolution," which seems so rapidly to have preëmpted the field, and which interprets the old Darwinian theory in such wise as to make it the foundation for a vigorous belief in the God and Father of Jesus Christ, a principle is emphasized which suggests the true relation of getting on to getting honor. At every stage of development already existing stuffs combine in such a way that a new element emerges, needing them to support it but wholly different from them and more significant. Molecules emerge from, require to be constituted by, but are different from, and have more possibilities than, atoms.

Solids emerge from, require the basis of, but are different from, and have more powers than, molecules. So life emerges from solids; mind from life; reason from mind; and finally spirit emerges from, needs the foundation of, but is different from, and better reflects reality than, reason. So we may roughly say that the idea of getting honor emerges from the ambition to get on, needs it for its incentive, but is different from it and of far greater ultimate importance. The person who puts getting on in first place is lower in the scale of being than the one who gives the precedence to getting honor.

This the gallant cavalier, Richard Lovelace, who was born to a fortune and could have enjoyed a life of ease on his own estate under the smile of his lady, well knew. When his king was in danger he recognized that there was only one thing for it: he gave his property and himself to the royalist cause, writing to his lady the celebrated lines,

> I could not love thee, dear, so much,
> Loved I not honor more.

This Moses also learned to know. He came to see that a true man cannot love the objects of his own desire at the expense of the objects of his fellow men's desire. One cannot love his own hearth and home truly except as it is encompassed by a love for the hearths and homes of all his countrymen. The wide love establishes the intense love. The love for one's fellow man, though diffused, crowns one's love for his own household, since it robs it of selfishness—and in happy love there is no self-ishness.

This is an answer to the question sometimes asked by those who have leanings toward the cults of free love. What is the necessity for the wedding service? May not two people found a home without benefit of church or justice of the peace? In a sense, possibly; but really, no. For such a union is unblessed by their fellow men. The minister at the wedding service reads, "Marriage is an honorable estate . . ." and that is exactly what it is. It is a state which receives the honor, the respect, of human society. The minister, representing society, blesses the pair, and they live in the midst of the good wishes of their kind. The bride and groom at a wedding acknowl-edge not only each other as husband and wife, but acknowledge also the society in which they live. It is a love, therefore, which expands in every direction. Affec-tion unites the two, and loyalty unites them both to their society. In the other sort of union there may be affection between the two, but there is no social loyalty. Their love is therefore boxed, limited, selfish—and the end of it is far likelier to be a shipwreck than that of the true marriage of good citizens, for the state of being cribbed and cabined is not natural to love, and is likely to warp it. Tolstoi thought that all such love was bound to bring up in some sort of misery. The heroine of his great novel declares her own feelings, after living a life spiritually disloyal to her society, by casting herself under the wheels of the train that carries her lover.

That person is wise who makes his getting on subservient to his getting honor, who follows his own desires only within the bounds of his social duties.

What I have been saying implies that *the standard of getting honor is made by the society in which we live.* Honor comes from our fellow men. To be sure, it is sometimes given where it is not due. Sometimes we give it to men of high financial station who, if the truth were known, are deceiving us, but that does not invalidate the truth that an honorable man is one who lives up to the best standards of his society.

If we had been standing with the father and son overlooking the city, we should not have been content with the description of human motives given by the two. We should have insisted on adding to the fact of selfish desire the unselfish loyalty of people to the ideals of their kind. No city, no nation, no world, could hold together and keep the peace even for a little if individual passion were the sole king of the human spirit. There is plainly another, a cohesive, force at work; and that is man-to-man loyalty, the social reward for which is honor. It is that pressure that keeps us engaged in honorable pursuits.

But it is to be feared that we might stop with this consideration. Self-expression and group loyalty, we might conclude, are the sum of human life. We might say with

(80)

Durkheim, that what people call their obligation toward God is in reality only our dimly felt and mistakenly interpreted obligation toward society. Society is to its members what God is to his worshipers. People have the burden upon them they themselves did not put there, that they must live up to this precept and that; and they spring to the conclusion that the burden is of God's making—when it is only society's. The difficulty with this social interpretation of religion is that it does not fit the religious consciousness. Often enough, to be sure, the will of God does accord with the will of society, but there comes a time when the two wills clash, and then true men know they must follow the unpopular and socially dishonorable course, if it be the will of God. Christ makes no hesitation and enjoins us to make none; he will go to the cross, that social stumbling-block and offense, and he will go in the face of the anger and fear of the whole contemporary race of men; he will go alone, as souls always go to meet their God; he will not meet the wishes of any of his society, but he will meet the wishes of his Father. Society does not look to religious persons like a god; it looks to them like a chaos which needs the brooding power of God upon it to bring it into cosmos.

There is one historical instance, pointed out by Dr. Grensted, when the human race—or the most important part of it—definitely adopted the philosophy that the only God there is is the human race itself, and the short life of that philosophy should be an example for all time. In the Roman Empire they attempted to erect an imperial cultus of "Roma et Augustus." In every city and village was set up the statue or some other symbol of the governing emperor. Every man was to bow his head to it as he passed by. The spirit of the Empire was to become the object of universal worship. But the whole world of loyal Roman citizens, pagan and Christian alike, rejected that religion from the start with a decision that was final—until some of our own philosophers stopped reading history. Whether it were Christ or some pagan deity, men and women demanded a revelation of a most high God greater than any empire or emperor, and not an empty and unreal personification of a system. You will find what the Christians thought of the imperial cult by reading the thirteenth chapter of Revelation, which tells how the Beast set up his image to be worshiped.

There is something more to add to living. Some people are the incarnation of personal desire; they believe in getting on. Others lift themselves up to a higher level; theirs is the comparative degree: they believe in getting honor as well as getting on; they refuse to get on if they cannot get honor; loyalty to their fellow men means more to them than license for themselves. But there are others who go farther still; theirs is the *superlative* degree; they believe in getting honest before God as well as in getting honor before their fellow men and getting on in their own ambitions; they refuse to get on or to get honor if they cannot get honest before God. And their lives acquire a certain fullness and balance which is not given on the lower levels of existence.

For, mark you, no person can truly love his fellows and do his best for them who does not love God more. The man who is thoroughly immersed in the spirit of his own group may be a most loyal member of it, but if he has nothing more in him than that spirit, how can he lift the group to higher things? The reason David Livingstone could bring light to the Dark Continent was because he came from a more enlightened continent. The reason the teacher can cause the child to grow in knowledge is because he comes to the child from the vast country of books and learning. Now if you live in your generation merely as a member in good and regular standing, you will be to it as the natives to Africa, or a child is to children; but if you come to it laden with thoughts of heaven, with intimations of eternal righteousness, with faith in the ultimate truth—if you come from an acquaintance with God and God's kingdom, then you have wherewith to lift it Godward. The more you love the Eternal, the more you have to give your fellow men.

But whether or not this were true, *it is our very nature to seek our highest standards not in ourselves nor in our society, but in God.* There is no rest for our yearning souls save in him. The only reason that people are religious at all is because there is a demand upon them they themselves did not invent that they be religious. There is nothing in the finite world as such that could have teased the generations of men to be uncontent with the finite. Only the Eternal could have wrought to such an effect. In his will alone is our peace, said Dante, and he said it for us all.

So the complete man is he who relaxes upon the everlasting arms. Sometimes the tremor running down those arms will cause a man to stand and denounce the very generation which brought him forth and in which he lives, an Athanasius against the world. It may almost be said that if you are not the champion of *some* unpopular cause or other, the hand of God is not upon you; for society is not perfect as the Father is perfect. But because of the everlasting arms, the complete man has a foundation for his life; the very grace of the Almighty enters into his living; he lives with a will because he knows that God's universe will not finally laugh at him.

Moses was not always the man who enjoyed that ultimate quality of honesty toward God. There was a time when the people had no water to drink and God told him where he might find it. And then, instead of giving God the glory, he took the credit to himself. He was all for the honor, but lacked the honesty.

But when honesty came to him, the friendship of God came, too. There is no description of any man in the Bible which one could more earnestly crave for himself than that of Moses which is given in my text, "Moses, whom the Lord knew face to face."

You can hardly have forgotten the moving scene in *The Green Pastures* when Moses takes leave of the Children of Israel he has led so long and loved so well. He is worn out and almost blind. Reluctantly he gives the command to go ahead, the leaders bid him farewell, the company marches on into the distance, and the old man is left alone. Not quite alone. God is there. He walks up to Moses and puts his hands on his shoulders.

Says Moses, "You's with me, ain't you, Lawd?"

And God says: "Co'se I is."

It has been worth while to be honest toward God.

VIII

IS GOD A PERSON?

A Sermon for Those Whose God Is Dead

*"God is a person: and they that worship him
must worship him in person and in truth."*
John 4:24

THESE are the words which Jesus spoke to the woman
at the well in Samaria. In our King James version we find
the word *spirit* used instead of *person*; but to convey the
real meaning of Jesus to our modern ears doubtless the
latter word is more pertinent. *Spirit* today calls up con-
notations of ghosts and unreality, whereas the evolution
of thought has impregnated the word *person* with the
ideas of consciousness and purpose—and that is probably
just the meaning that Jesus meant to convey. God knows
himself and his world, and has a purpose for the latter.
There is no faculty that you or I have that God has not.
He is a person.

Come now, one will ask, is God such a person as I
am? Has he legs, arms, and a face as primitive people
have thought that he had and as the medieval artists sometimes depicted him as having? Manifestly not, but neither

(86)

are any of these properties essential to personality. If
you lose your leg you do not cease to be a person; if
you lose your arm you do not reduce yourself to the
category of a thing: the features of your face may be
distorted in an accident, but you still remain yourself.
Even your brain is not you, but only another instrument
you employ to apprehend the world around you. All
these things are external to the essential you—to that
which you refer to when you say "I."

Our question is now quite simple: can God say "I"
as we say it?—*I* will, *I* will not? I do not ask that we
should say it in English (though we have it on the best
authority that he is Nordic in his tastes and has given
up his former predilection for the Jews). It is enough
that he should be able to say "I" in his own language,
and so launch his purposes in the world. And this is just
what Jesus announces that he can do. He *is* a person.

But instantly I hear the protest of a long line of men
who cannot believe that he is a person. Not far from
the head of the historical procession is Ecclesiastes, whose
thoughts on the subject are well known: "As the fishes
that are taken in an evil net, and as the birds that are
caught in a snare, so are the sons of men snared in an
evil time, when it falleth suddenly upon them." To him
the world seemed like a great net whose meshes are
physical circumstances. There are persons in the world,
to be sure, you and I and the others, but we are inclosed

in an infinite framework of impersonal forces which take no thought and cherish no purpose for us because there is no thought or purpose in them. Men and women have come into being in this insensible milieu by chance, sheer chance.

The long unhappy line of the doubting continues until this day. There is, to be sure, not nearly so much skepticism among our novelists today as there was a decade ago, but the mood of Ecclesiastes is never far from some of them. One contemporary writer, looking with his hero at the waves on the beach, reflects upon this "great rhythm of ordered accident. The sea, the silly sea, meaningless, prolific, brawling over the cold pumice reefs of dead volcanoes, groping up slants of thirsty sand. The sea, the bitter sea, that makes man suspect he is homeless." Here again is the same imagery; in the center, life, intelligence, persons—but all about, the expanse of physical forces—a sea, a silly sea, meaningless, having no final gift but death.

According to this picture, in its ancient as well as its modern presentation, the universe is a dynamic but blind thing, on a kind of island in the midst of which have grown up persons who possess intelligent purposes, all of whom await alike the inevitable hour. The path of ignominy as well as glory leads but to the grave.

The picture in the mind of Christ was wholly unlike this. Instead of conceiving existence as surrounded by a sea of meaningless forces, he felt the arms of God under all and saw the eye of God above all. There are certainly such things as physical forces and material bodies, but these are not primary; they derive from the creative will of God. God owns them. Earth—it is God's footstool. Jerusalem—it is his city. Behold the fowls of the air, for they sow not, neither do they reap, nor gather into barns; yet your heavenly Father feedeth them. Consider the lilies of the field, how they grow; they toil not, neither do they spin, and yet I say unto you that even Solomon in all his glory was not arrayed like one of these—and it is God who clothes them. Such was Christ's world.

This picture is to Ecclesiastes' as a negative to a positive print: where he sees darkness, Christ sees light, and where he fancies he sees light Christ sees darkness—for Christ finds no pleasure, as the Preacher does, in the mere fact of being alive. To Christ all of life—your life, mine—is supported and suffused by the purpose of God. And the forces purposeless in themselves, the winds, the waves, electricity and all the circumstances of time, not excepting the circumstance of death, these are used by the Father for his own good ends. For Christ, God's purpose brings forth and employs the non-purposive: he would never have dreamed of believing that the non-purposive could somehow conceive and bring forth creatures of purpose. It is not we who are remote in nature from the power which sustains life; it is the things of the earth that cannot know him.

No one ever drew a more utterly personal picture of existence than Christ. He saw the world as a home, and all the persons in it as the members of one family. The children of the family—mankind—were wont to do wrong. Wrong-doing is any act which results in breaking up the family spirit of the world. Men resisted the loving purpose of God as individuals and by societies. In Christ's day they let little selfish animal motives dominate them —as we do in our day. In his day they made war, man against man—just as we do. In his day men climbed to privilege and power over the broken bodies of their competitors, exploited women and children, refused to take seriously the challenge to build a new society—even as you and I. It was because the children of the family— mankind—in that day and this had done wrong that the Father of the family had to punish them. And this he did, and does, through what we have come to call social and economic laws. Man-to-man justice tends to lead to prosperity, and injustice to trouble. As the old wars brought their own ruin in their wake, so do our new wars, whether economic or military, for God is not mocked. Our sin still finds us out.

But there was an Elder Brother in that family, and he and his Father went in compassion and tears to that needy people in their due suffering. They made themselves one with them in their pains and punishments, as a shepherd makes his own the distress of a lost sheep for which he searches in the wilderness. The Elder

Brother risked himself to save the people from their own wrong-doing and its results, but the very wickedness he came to eradicate flew at him and finally slew him. The way he lived and the way he died revealed at once the blackness of men's sin against God's clear purpose and the brightness of God's love for man.

Such was the picture of history Christ painted—from first to last a picture of persons—and he painted it not on any ordinary canvas nor with ordinary colors, but on the rough fabric of history itself, drawing his lighter shades from the sunshine on the shore of Galilee and the darker from the earthquake and the loneliness of Golgotha.

So you have the two pictures purporting to represent things as they are. The one shows purposelessness as the basic element, in the bosom of which people who think and hope and carry a purpose upon them have somehow come into being. The other shows as the basis of all things a God of fatherly purposes, who has brought into life persons who can love, be loved by him, and do his gracious will, and who has made also a vast complex of forces called the physical universe which serves him at its own level.

For those who see life in this latter guise the skeptic has an explanation or two ready.

You believe in a personal God, says he, not because he is objectively real, but because you wish to believe in him. Your thought is not realistic enough to overcome the fantasies thrown up by your hidden wishes. Your emotions do your thinking for you.

It is to be acknowledged that "wishful thinking" is one of the subtlest and most pernicious evils to which the human mind is heir. But the mere fact that one's wishes and one's thoughts agree is not sufficient to prove that the thinking is the result of the wishing. I wish to believe in the sun because it gives life, in the stars because they make the night beautiful, in man because he is both affecting and majestic. I also think that sun, stars, and man exist. In this case the wish to believe is obviously no father to the thought. Neither is it necessarily so in the case of God: my undeniable wish to believe in him does not necessarily stamp him as unreal.

True religion condemns thinking that is merely wishful no less than skepticism does. The whole burden of the Old Testament prophets is that the people believed in the gods they liked to believe in, instead of the most high God of inflexible justice and truth. The far from skeptical Socrates spent his life delving into the minds of his contemporaries, exposing the selfish desires they substituted for convictions. Indeed, the very reason that religion condemns certain forms of skepticism is because they are themselves expressions of wishful thinking. It is well known that a man attempting to compensate for an inferiority complex may become an atheist. Here is a way to assert oneself with a vengeance. The denial of

God is one of the easiest means of fulfilling one's wish to be conspicuous among one's fellows. It might be called wishful thinking *par excellence*. Witness the play of forces in Eugene O'Neill's powerful drama, "Days Without End," in which the hero finally comes to himself by discovering that his negative philosophy has been only the cloak for a selfish subconscious desire to flout the universe and its crowning principle, love.

A second skeptical explanation of the belief of man in a personal God is that the belief, if not a projection of one's own wish, represents at least the wish of the society he lives in. When, for instance, men believed in the divine right of kings, their faith evidently reflected the desire of their generation to perpetuate monarchy. So now the belief in a God of eternal justice who will punish the wrong-doer reflects merely the unthought-out desire of our age to establish what we deem to be "right" laws and keep our particular type of civilization going.

But, as Professor Brightman says, this explanation is hardly thoroughgoing enough. If the idea of a God eternally just is simply a device to support the law courts, we shall have to go farther and say that science, with the alleged augustness of its own principles, is merely a complex of social wishes directed toward keeping busy the universities, the learned societies, and the booksellers. And no modern philosopher with a sense of humor would quite go to that limit.

The fact is that religion, so far from being a product

of the social wish, has more than once been the very
force in history which has challenged and overthrown
the ideas of its society, and furnished the seeds of new
social conceptions. The democratic feeling implicit in
Christianity had no little to do with relegating the doctrine of the divine right of kings into limbo; and today
where can we look with more certainty for a radical
condemnation of unbridled capitalism, the war system,
and all the rest of the luggage of the general contemporary mind than to the church?

The only good explanation of why the idea of a personal God entered the mind of man is similar to the explanation of why the idea of the sun or of any other
natural object entered our thought. The idea was not
an invention either individual or social, but an acknowl-
edgment of a reality.

Those who know God have, on their part, an explanation as to why skeptics believe that physics has the last
word about existence. The latter, say they, stand off and
philosophize about life; they do not permit themselves
to become so immersed in it as to know it with spiritual
immediacy. The physical senses, which are not the only
channels for apprehending reality, can give them only a
fragmentary view. Skeptics *look* at life, and it does *look*
material.

It looks black and dead, like the ocean at night. But
the swimmer who dives into a bay of ocean knows that

it is neither black nor dead. The darker the night, the better: he finds himself, in his plunge, in the midst of light, for the water glows with phosphorescence. It covers him with brilliance as with a garment, shining the brighter where he swims the more strenuously.

There is no argument or explanation to convince any of us of the personality of God; but if we wish to know that personality, we have only to cast ourselves completely into life. His will, which informs life, becomes luminous where it touches one. As the bather sees himself limned in brightness by the resistance of the water, so, by what the mystics call the glow of the spirit, one becomes aware of what Dr. Farmer names the value-resistances of God. You have not begun to be immersed in life until you feel these. But if you allow yourself to be sensitive to them, the way begins to open into the knowledge that the God whose will animates the world is as personal as you or I. Doubtless he is more than a person, as we know persons, but if he were not at least a person, how could he touch our wills with such exquisite immediateness?

"It is told of Aggrey, the African Negro Christian, descended from a line of proud chieftains, that once at breakfast he spoke hurtingly to his wife in the presence of her sister. That night God met his proud spirit in a tremendous value-resistance. He must apologize and set the matter right. Very well, he would do it quietly and privately. Then God resisted that. The apology must be in the presence of the sister, for she too had been present and was involved, therefore, in the jangled personal relationship. All night long God wrestled with Aggrey's imperious nature, and won. At breakfast the next day Aggrey apologized unconditionally to both women, who, knowing his nature, were almost in tears at such a humble giving away of self to them. Surely at that table all most livingly felt, as never before or elsewhere, the overshadowing reality of God—of God, not as a vague cosmic force to be worshiped in vague, adulatory phrases, but as Personal Purpose working recreatively and insistently."— (Dr. Herbert H. Farmer.)

This was a time of crisis for Aggrey, but we should miss the meaning of God's hand upon us if we supposed that he came to us and that we might be aware of his purpose upon us only in times of crisis. We live with God constantly, and he lives with us. Is there any moment when he is not summoning you to turn from your second-best to your best? Any moment when he does not call you to seek and to create that which is beautiful and good? Well do they know who have lived life deeply that God *can* say "I *will*" and "I *will not*"—and that he does say both. The effect of the impact of God's person upon any man is to move him up and away from the merely material elements in life and toward the highest personality. The man thus moved comes to know an eternal secret, that in the mysterious fabric of the universe, the warp out of which all lives are woven is not purposelessness, but God. He is ready joyously to say with Christ, "God is a person: and they that worship him must worship him in person and in truth."

I know my God to be—
What He knows me to be—
Alive.

Have you never wrestled with Him,
Never felt the muscle of His arm
In wind or tide or mountain-steep?
Never striving drawn strength from Him?

Have you never matched minds with Him,
Never searched His secret in atom or in star,
Never known the pain of infinite thinking?

Have you never been still,
Never been aware, before Him,
As He breathed an ideal
In on your soul?

Go to your God:
Ask Him to come to you
Alive.

IX

WHAT IS TRUE FORGIVENESS?

A Sermon for Hard Folk

*"Then came Peter to him [to Jesus], and said,
Lord, how oft shall my brother sin against me,
and I forgive him? Till seven times?"*
MATT. 18:21

IF JESUS had been an ordinary rabbi, he would have had
an ordinary answer ready. He might have said, as Rabbi
Jose ben Jehuda actually did say, "If a man commits an
offense once, . . . forgive him; a second time, . . . forgive him; a third time, . . . forgive him; the fourth time,
. . . do not forgive him." To pardon a man more than
three times for a repeated offense seemed to be asking
too much of human nature.

But Jesus was no ordinary rabbi. He gave a new answer, putting it in words which could not but have re-
minded his hearers of the famous boast of Lamech in the
Old Testament, "If Cain shall be avenged sevenfold, truly
Lamech seventy and sevenfold." Lamech's idea was that
if a man did him wrong he should take infinite—for the
combination of the sevens stands for something infinite
—vengeance upon him. The truth which Jesus set up

against this outworn idea was the exact opposite of it. A man should not take vengeance on one who wrongs him at all; he should forgive him instead; and he should forgive him not merely three times, as certain rabbis said, nor seven times, as Peter suggested his answer might be, but an infinite number of times, as the combination of the sevens again implies. "I say not unto thee, Until seven times; but, Until seventy times seven."

Then follows the wonderfully modern parable about the infinite forgiveness of God and that of men. To appreciate its modernity it is necessary only to reduce the "talents" and "pence" to dollars. Since silver has been selling recently for about forty cents an ounce, the story should be understood to read:

An industrialist owed a bank an enormous sum—three million dollars. He went to the president of the bank, told him he could not pay the sum, and had the debt most favorably readjusted. An employee owed him exactly five dollars. He went to him and demanded his money. When the employee told him he could not pay it, he fired him.

We have our own name for a man like that, as did those to whom Jesus first spoke the parable. It is our universal human antipathy to the kind of man who will accept favors he will not give that lends the story its pointedness in every age. God is infinitely forgiving toward us: the ideal for us in relation to our fellows is plain.

What! one will say, are we to go on and on forgiving

people who wrong us, asking from them no restitution and no evidence of repentance?

Such a question makes it clear that we ought to look carefully into what Christ meant by forgiveness. As one can see from the very etymology of the word, to forgive means to overgive, to give more than is deserved. In our more specific application of it it means to give up a rightful claim against a wrong-doer. Shall we then give up such claims out of hand, without asking any questions or making any demands? If a husband wrongs his wife, should she forgive him without further ado? If a supposed friend steals property from you, should you forgive him without waiting for so much as an "I am sorry" on his part? The answer is unequivocal: yes! three times, yes! seven times, yes! forever, yes!—if you understand forgiveness as Christ taught it.

Renan perfectly expressed the mind of Christ when he said, "There is only one problem, and that is interior." Jesus consecrated his life to the truth that the human heart is the arena where, if anywhere, good must vanquish evil. If goodness cannot be established there, it is foolish to attempt to establish it elsewhere in the world. Given right motives, right social adjustments will follow: the problem is to establish right motives within oneself.

Jesus' teaching about forgiveness penetrates straight to this inner area of the soul. To forgive is to waive the motive of vengeance, however deserving of punishment

67028

a wrong-doer may be. To forgive is to give up resentment against a person, however rightful, according to
ordinary standards, resentment would be. To forgive is
to turn to a wrong-doer, as the heroine of Gertrude
Atherton's *The Mansion*, turns to her husband, after he
has crept back to her home a guilty soul and laid bare
his disloyalty to her. He knows he deserves nothing from
her; he expects nothing, save to be told to look for his
living in the gutter, where he belongs; but he feels he
must make his confession. After he has spoken, she is
silent, until, with wet eyes, her own heart being broken,
she turns to him and says: "I do not see yet how it will
be best to do it, but—you and I must work this out together." Forgiveness is keeping love uppermost in the
heart, even when hatred and anger and all the brood that
issue from one's sense of being wronged, wronged,
wronged, shout for vengeance.

Full and free forgiveness is not necessarily followed
by taking the wrong-doer back into the same environment in which he succumbed to temptation. It might be
no kindness to do so. It might only tend to confirm him
in his weakness. What follows forgiveness is the deter-
mination to see that done which is of greatest possible
benefit to the delinquent. How can it help a child to grow
in character if he is exposed, when still impressionable,
to the same set of forces which have already proved
too much for him? How can such a procedure help a

(101)

man or a woman? Forgiving a person involves doing right by him, whatever that right may be.

Easily said! But how rare is true forgiveness! Resentment is the natural reaction of the heart, and vengeance the accompaniment of it. Forgiveness costs. The price of it is too high for most of us.

Sometimes we are forced by events into a kind of forgiveness. A Scottish story tells of a man "who, fearing that he was on his death-bed, sent for an acquaintance with whom he had fallen out years before, and made overtures of peace. They shook hands in amity. But as the other left the room the sick man roused himself to say, 'Remember, if I get over this, the old quarrel stands.'"

True forgiveness is not forced from without; it is of the heart; but it is none the less attended with pain. It is something which must be created in face of circumstance—and all creation is painful. There is always a cross in forgiveness, a cross voluntarily taken up. There is a knowledge that you have been, consciously or unconsciously, despised by the one who has wronged you. The experience of knowing you have been unjustly dealt with is pure pain. It is out of sheer suffering that one has to lift his head, rededicate himself to love, and live out the words, "Father, forgive them; they know not what they do." If the one who has wronged you is quite indifferent to his fault and goes his way in the spirit of the contemporary saying, "There is no use worrying about one's sins," somebody else then will have to worry about them all the more, and in this case, since you are determined not to let your love for him fade, that somebody is you. You will begin to understand the meaning of Calvary better than if you had read all the theologians in the world on the subject. You will discern the significance of the saying that Hugh Mackintosh quotes from Horace Bushnell, that the doctrine of the cross is the doctrine of the cost of forgiveness to God. It is the doctrine of what it costs love to be injured and yet go on loving.

But forgiveness also happens to be the most—I was going to say the only—effective force for the redemption of one who has done the wrong.

The psychologists point out that when one has a burden of guilt on his mind, he unconsciously sets to work to bury it. He tries to forget it by hard work or a relentless round of pleasures. He compensates for it by developing a flinty manner or an over-aggressive one, toward other people. He builds up a set of fancies about himself and his possibilities which he mistakes for realities. And all this to be rid of realizing he has an inner burden —that guilt complex. The subconscious desire to be free from the realization changes, warps, and denatures his personality as he carries it through the years. Because he feels his real self has failed, he separates it from the world lest the world should see it as it is. So he becomes two selves, with tension between, and that means torture.

Then comes a friend, the very friend whom he has wronged. This friend has in him the same love that was in Christ. He says to the poor fellow fighting a losing fight with his guilt—says it in his own words: "Bill, I don't think you did right. You cut me to the quick. You'll never know how I felt it. But I want you to know one thing. I don't hold it against you. Doubtless you have been punished for it in nameless ways, for this is a just world, in its larger aspects. But so far as I am concerned, our friendship is just as green as it ever was. On the ground of it anything good can grow up. Let's plant some new seeds."

That is forgiveness—the readiness to start with the offender in a new beginning. It releases his real self once more. The consciousness of being forgiven dissolves the complex, for here is a friend, a part of the world outside him, who sees him as he is, and is yet ready to coöperate with him in a new life. Through that friendship his real self can return to the world. The inner self and the self shown the world merge once more: the tension is resolved: the soul is "integrated"; in forgiveness it comes to know the peace which is power and the power which is peace.

Forgiveness, therefore, implies giving the one who has done wrong a chance to make good. It is never a simple forgetting of the past; it is an opening to him of a future in which he may live down his past.

It is at this point, as Dr. Dinsmore has pointed out, that Milton is more discerning than Dante. Both poets were aware that the consciousness of having sinned, unless something were done about it, would remain a dead weight and source of agony to sinners who, repenting, entered heaven. The problem was how the mind of wrong-doers might be changed so that they could be happy in the last estate. This Dante solved in a quite arti-ficial way: the pardoned sinner was allowed to drink of the water of Lethe, which washed his memory clear of the sinful past. But actual life provides no such waters of Lethe. The only hope for one who has sinned is the chance to make his sin the point of departure from which he may set out to live as God would have him. Milton pictures Adam, after the Fall, prostrated by the thought of his sin and its consequences. There seems no refuge for him from the crushing thought, *I willed the evil in the world*. But at last he finds comfort. From the moun-tain top he is allowed to look into the future: there he sees how Christ, the second Adam, the ideal of his better self, overcomes the evil with good. He comes down from the mountain with his heart filled with peace from the thought, *I now will that which will one day conquer evil*.

Jesus never failed to let people know that the future can overcome the past. He gave all whom he met a redemptive hope. Three pictures from his life, which might be abundantly multiplied, show three different types of hope he imparted, but each one of them a hope to make good.

A woman stood in the midst of a group of threatening men. They accused her, before Jesus, of breaking one of the cardinal laws of Moses. They were for stoning her to death, and whether they followed this course or not, she must have considered herself a doomed woman, for she knew that from now on she should be an outcast. She would not be allowed to worship in the church nor enter a reputable home. There was no circumstance to suggest that she might ever again return to a life of normal happiness. She had had her chance—and was a failure. She was chained to her past. So she could not but have thought.

Then Jesus acted. His command to the men put affairs in their proper light: "He that is without sin, let him first cast a stone at her." The Scripture has it that "they which heard, being convicted by their own conscience, went out one by one, beginning at the eldest, even unto the last." The air was cleared, and the woman saw herself free, the restraints and menace of her past life, represented in the men who surrounded her, completely done away. Jesus, forgiving her, gave her a sense of individual possibility.

Another picture. Jesus had a sudden strange influence

over Zaccheus. On the way through Jericho, he had been
welcomed to the home of the wealthy tax-gatherer, and
had spent a happy hour or more conversing with him
and his household. Now his host dramatically arose and
announced: "I hereby give half of all I possess to the
poor; and to any man whom I have cheated out of anything I will give back four times as much."

If by cheating is meant deceiving, Zaccheus had not
been cheating anybody, for everyone took it for granted
that the tax-collector's business was to exact as much
as he could from the people within his jurisdiction.
Cicero had said that it was necessary for the men at the
top of the system to make three fortunes, one to pay
in to the government, one to meet a series of charges of
extortion in the courts, and one to live on after all other
bills were paid.

It was the system itself that was iniquitous. This farm-
ing of the taxes, that is, the paying of a fixed sum for the
privilege, in a certain territory, of raising in taxes all
the money one could, obviously carried in itself all the
seeds of malfeasance. On the other hand, Rome felt, and
probably on good grounds, that the people at large were
ready to cheat the government on any pretext, and that
the only way to meet dishonesty on the part of the citizens was by dishonesty on the part of the officials. Fight
fire with fire. One may imagine Zaccheus many days
of his life wishing himself out of the system, and as often,

after reflecting that it had the whole tradition of Rome behind it and universal recognition throughout the world, concluding that it simply could not be changed, and that certainly he as an individual was not the one to attempt to change it.

Then Jesus talked to him and he made his sudden declaration. He had been lifted to a believing-point that the system was not rigidly unchangeable. Jesus, forgiving him, gave him a sense of social possibility.

There is a third picture: that of three crosses on a hill. One of the men crucified there had been a thief. If his career had been like that of many thieves, he could have had virtually no chance for honest living whatever. His parentage and his surroundings, we may imagine, had opened to him the profession of thievery as a course without alternative. Cradled and reared in ignorance and vice, he had never dreamed of any but a degraded life. Possibly he was mentally unmatured or diseased, so that he could not adjust himself to decent social life. It is all very well to maintain that we should live up to our natural possibilities, but here was a man without any whatever.

But even to him Jesus imparted a hope. "Today," he said, "shalt thou be with me in paradise." Jesus, forgiving him, gave him a sense of eternal possibility.

Some one will be saying, Ah, if only I myself were

more forgiving! But how can I cultivate that power? Our parable suggests the answer: the best way to save ourselves from a wrong attitude to the man who owes us the little debt is to keep ourselves aware of the attitude of God—to whom we owe more than a little debt— to us.

When you know that however "down" you are, you are not "out" in the sight of God; when you inventory all your assets of opportunity, given you all out of the love of the Creator, and not for any desert of your own, since fundamentally you are not the source of your own existence; when you hear without hearing the still small voice which bids you look up and not down, forward and not back, to eternity and not time; when this experience is yours even *after* you have known you do not deserve it—that is forgiveness. And it is just that which may be so strangely creative in your own life. It lays upon you a standard for living which is alive. The way of God with you suggests with an urgency and anticipation which may not be denied your perfect way with your fellow men. Neither must *they* be "out," however down they be! Did God turn away from you?— neither will you turn away from those who have wronged you.

When the human soul is confronted in its sin by the Great Forgiver there comes to it the infinitely painful-joyous sense of deserving nothing and yet desiring to

deserve. One stands before Him like the soldier described
by Studdert Kennedy,[1]

> And then at last he said one word,
> He just said one word—"Well?"
> And I said in a funny voice,
> "Please can I go to Hell?"
>
> . . . .
>
> "You can't, that Hell is for the blind,
> And not for those that see.
> You know that you have earned it, lad,
> So you must follow Me."

[1] From "Well?" in *The Sorrows of God and Other Poems*, by
Studdert Kennedy. By permission of the publisher, Harper &
Brothers.

X

L'ENVOI: THE LAST MOMENT ON THE CROSS

A Sermon for Everyone

"Father, into Thy hands I commend my spirit. . . ."
LUKE 23:46

Now was the ultimate time. Up till now he might, if he would, have taken refuge in the conditional mood: *if* God wills it, then I must die—or at least in an ameliorating future tense: I *will* die, but not yet. Now, however, he had arrived at the prodigious moment. He knew that all there was to be said was the stark and simple terribleness of the words, a minute more and my life is done.

The choice was too poignantly clean cut—to surrender himself either in one direction or the other.

On the one hand, there was the world before him, still vivid and alive to his dimming eyes. It was a satanic world. The devil, as a roaring lion, goeth about seeking whom he may devour, and now the lion was about to make his kill. The crowd *was* like a lion. It raged and roared about him. There, dressed in striped tunics, were some of the wealthier men of the city, holding as aloof

(111)

as possible from the wretched rabble of the slums. Wealthy with gold in hand, heavy with hate in heart. There were the villagers whom the festival had brought to the city with their families, farm hands dressed in bagging, shepherds dressed in goatskins, lines of hardness, accentuated by the occasion, visible under the sweat and dirt of their faces. There were the Roman legionaries, thin-lipped and sneering, one of them ready with his spear to strike to see if there were an answering quiver.

Not the crowd only; the whole world was like a lion. Existence seemed hungry with a blind cruel hunger. It was a thing of fangs and maw. One might have expected intelligence from the world; his brain teemed with ideas he had not yet imparted to his generation—but life did not seem interested in ideas; it had dragged him from experience to experience until now it was brutishly to let him die. One might have expected a little justice in the world. He had given his best, walked up and down the country till his feet were sore, teaching the people the secret of life; but life did not seem interested in one's best. For one's best it indifferently returned its worst. Its was a savage beast-spirit. One might have expected a dash of friendship. There had been friendship up till the last. One or two of the disciples had seemed really to understand him. Had not the good Peter said, If I must die with thee, I will not deny thee! And now Peter was skulking to safety out of the city gate. In the last analysis life was against him: it had no more regard for him than a monster would. It was essentially selfish: it did not care; and it finally dealt out death to everything, even the best. It was the kingdom of Satan: it was ruled by the roaring lion.

Everything he saw before his eyes suggested that view of life. It was the logical, even necessary thing for him to accept it, and to die with the cry on his lips: Selfishness is king; nothing is saved for its own sake; time is a maniac flinging fire—and to its claim I surrender my spirit.

But Jesus' life consisted not only of that which he saw before his eyes. He had the will of God in his heart. He hung, as a matter of fact, between two sets of forces: before him, the selfish forces of earth, savage, beastly; behind him—behind his will, behind his mind—the will of God, the things of heaven. The altar-piece painted by Mathias Grünewald for the monastery chapel of Isenheim, Germany, illustrates his state. This is a type of reredos common in the Middle Ages, with double wings which fold over upon and conceal it, offering the artist the decoration not only of the central panel itself and the interior surface of the open wings, but also the exterior surface of the closed wings. As you look at the Grünewald altar when closed, your eye is held by the imposing figure of the son of man crucified. He hangs there on a rough-hewn cross against a sky opaque with darkness, and all about him are the crowd who have hounded him to his death. On holy days, however, the altar was opened—and what a contrast! Here are scenes not of earth, but of heaven; and dominating all, in the midst of a golden light and the flashing pinions of ten thousand angels, "one feels rather than sees" the presence of the Father. Christ literally hangs there between God, unseen to the ordinary eye, but as close behind him as conscience, and the world, the selfish, death-bound world.

The Christ who actually died upon the cross knew well enough that there were forces in life besides those vicious ones that he saw before him. Was there not something in his life that had told him it was good to take the little children and bless them, to forgive the woman taken in sin, to seek and to save all who were lost? This will was a good will, forever good. Mercy was better than vengeance; love was better than hate; heroic sacrifice was better than selfish cowardice. This he knew in his heart.

So he had to decide which was eternal and which temporary—the will of the lion he saw in the world, or the will he knew in his heart. Which was of God? There was no real choice for him. He deeply knew the will of God. And he said, in utter spiritual relaxation, Father, into thy hands I commend my spirit.

So perfectly did he surrender to the will of God that to us he is the embodiment of that will. For us today the choice is more vivid. Whereas he had to decide between the vividness of the lion-like forces of material life and the *seeming* unreality of the will of God within him, we have the two palpable pieces of evidence to choose from—the clearly seen world and the clearly seen Christ. Selfishness and selflessness—the lion and the Lamb.

We have seen the effect of the lion and the Lamb in real life. We have seen the wars, the sins, the wretchedness that the forces of materialism produce. But we have seen also what the Lamb has done: when men have adopted the spirit of Christ they have built the hospitals, they have brought the races together, they have achieved peace for great areas in the world and will finally do so for the whole world. We have seen the actual effect on material reality that the dedication to the will of the caring, loving, immortal God has had. History has made it easier for us to know which represents the eternal will of God—the selfish, lion-like forces of the world which result in death, or the unselfish forces in which there is care and love. The choice is to be made.

What then do you do? Do you say, "O satanic god of the forces of selfishness and death: you are the all and in-all, and to you I surrender my spirit." Or looking at Christ, do you see the greater power and say, with him, "Father, into thy hands I commend my spirit"?

Both the lion and the Lamb are hunting you. The truth is expressed in the vivid words of Ruth Temple Lindsay,

TAKING A CITY

The lion, he prowleth far and near,
  Nor swerves for pain or rue;
He heedeth naught of sloth nor fear,
  He prowleth—prowleth—through
The silent glade and the weary street,
  In the empty dark and the full noon heat;
And a little Lamb with aching Feet—
  He prowleth too.

The lion, he strayeth near and far;
  What heights hath he left untrod?
He crawleth nigh to the purest star
  On the trail of the saints of God.

The lion croucheth alert, apart—
  With patience doth he woo;
He waiteth long by the shuttered heart,
  And the Lamb—He waiteth too.
Up the lurid passes of dreams that kill,
  Through the twisting maze of the great untrue,
The lion followeth the fainting will—
  But the Lamb—*He followeth too*.

THE END